Feathered Critter Friends
Vol. I

Feathered Critter Friends
Vol. I

Rob Benton

Esotericom®

All birds depicted herein were photographed in the course of their natural behavior. No bird was enticed, confined, entrapped, or harassed in any way in the making of these photographs.

Captions indicate general identification of the bird and where the photograph was made.

Front Cover: Fairy Wren, Western Australia
Back Cover: White-Throated Kingfisher, Singapore

All photographs by Rob Benton

ISBN 978-0-9710702-7-1

AND GOD SAID , "LET THE WATERS BRING FORTH SWARMS OF LIVING CREATURES, AND LET BIRDS FLY ABOVE THE EARTH ACROSS THE FIRMAMENT OF THE HEAVENS."

GENESIS 1:20

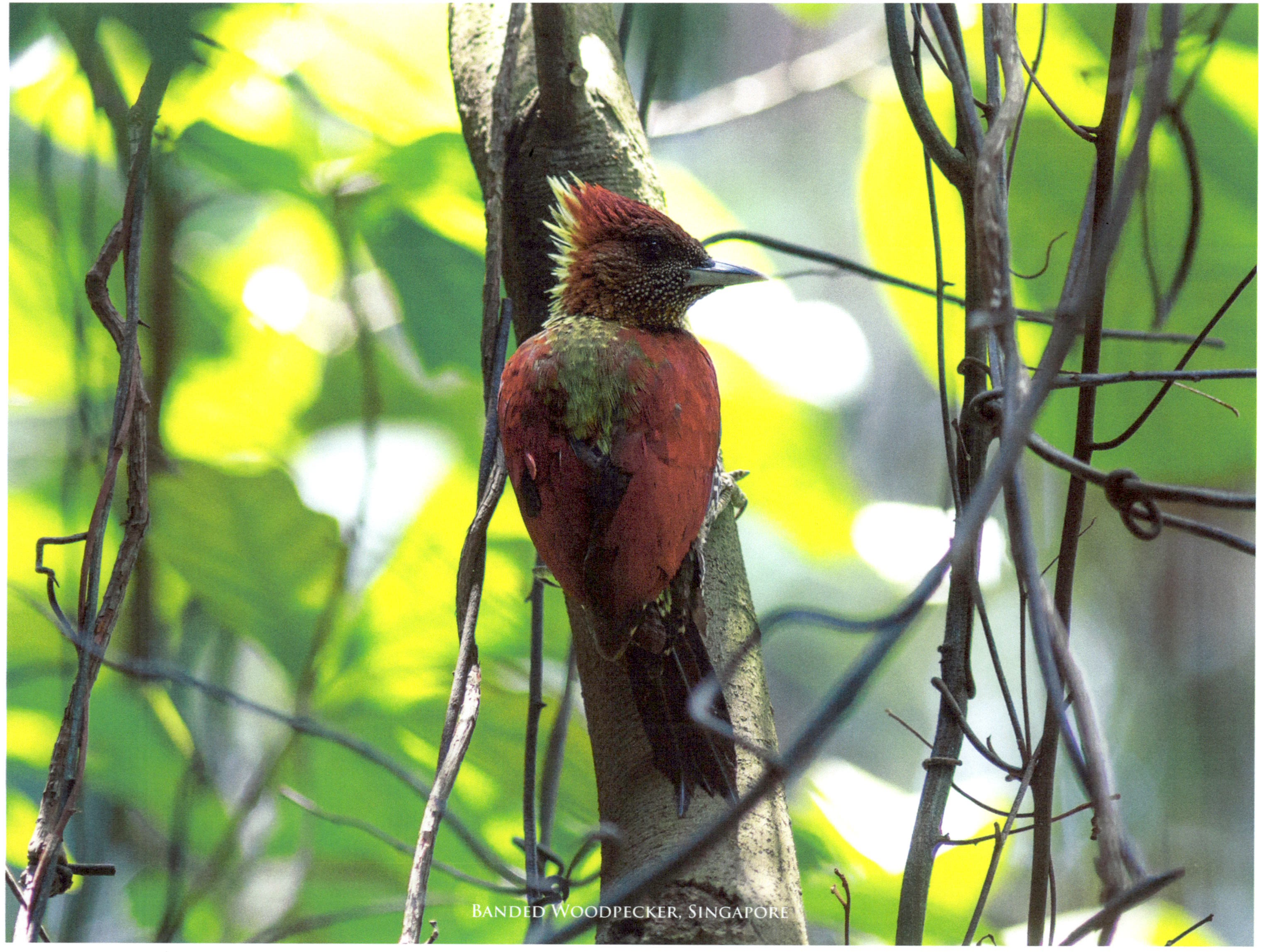

Banded Woodpecker, Singapore

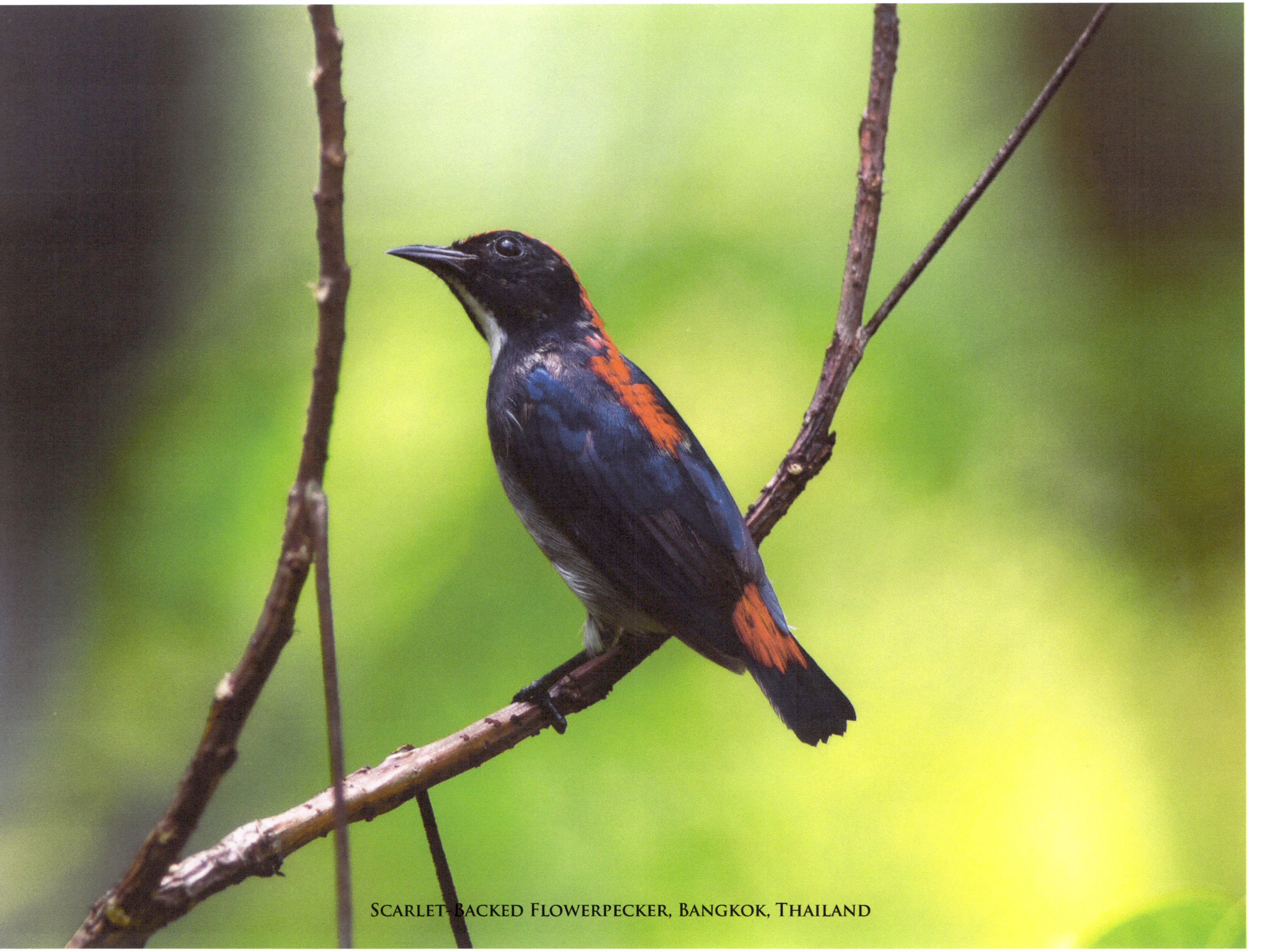

Scarlet-backed Flowerpecker, Bangkok, Thailand

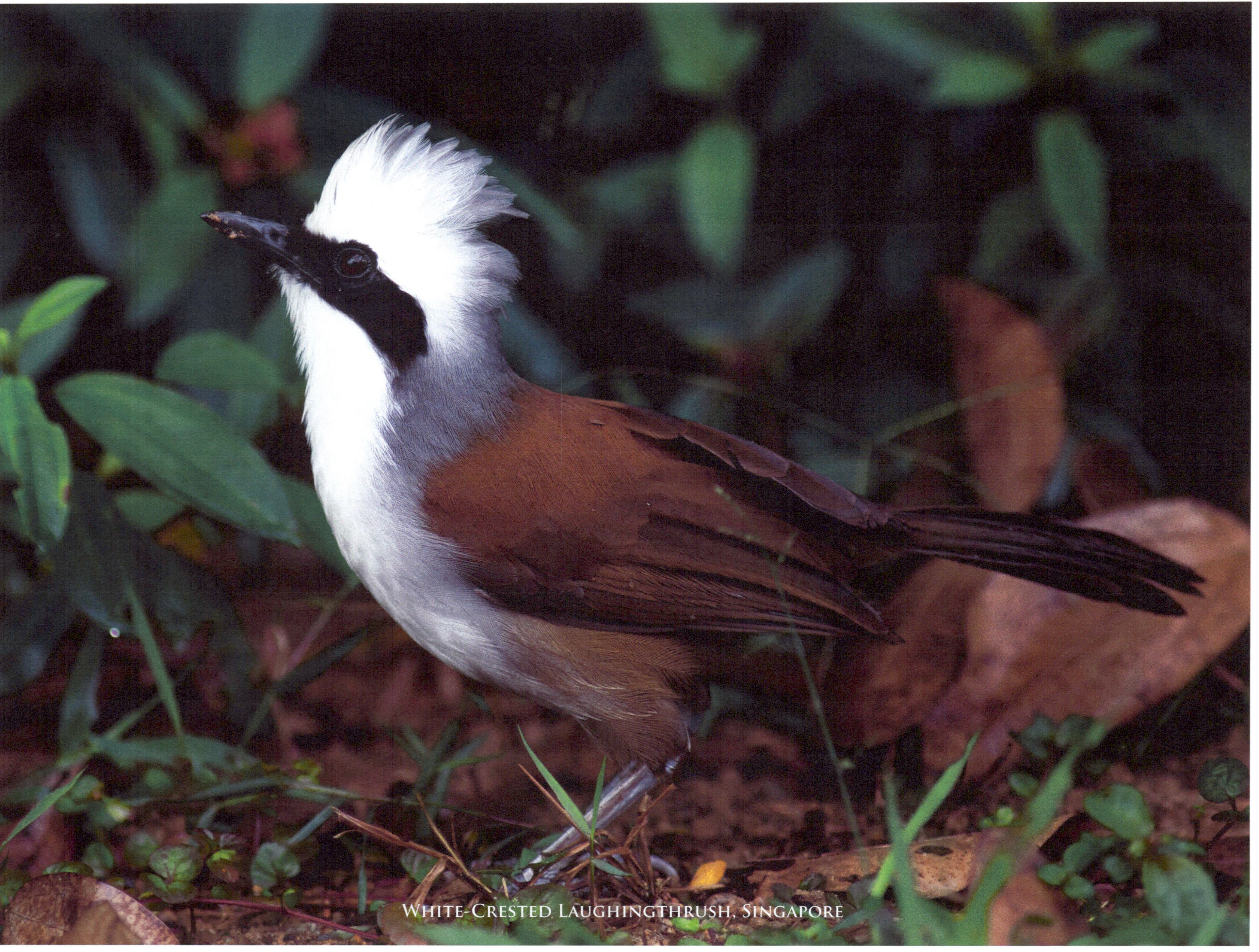

White-Crested Laughingthrush, Singapore

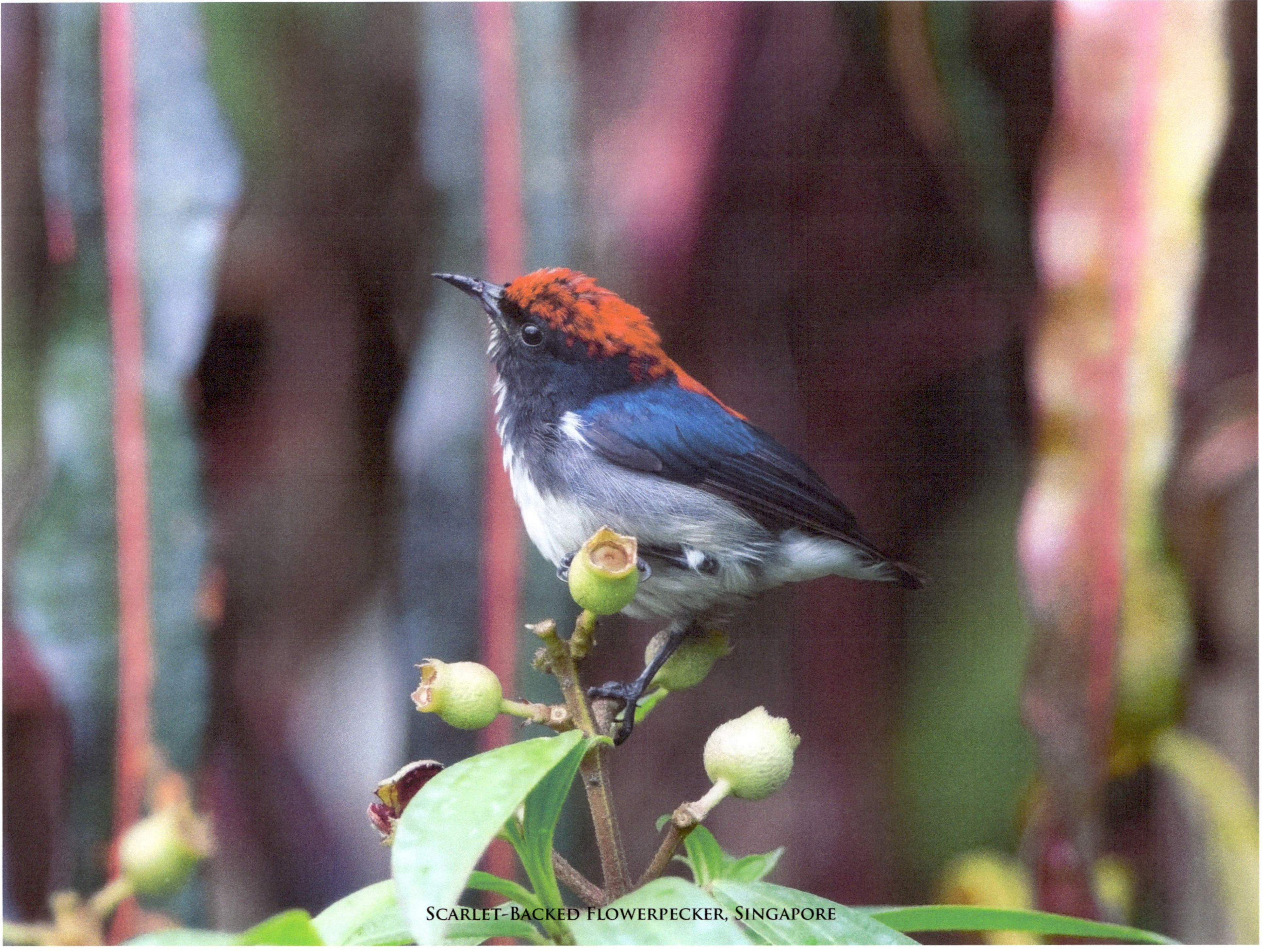

Scarlet-Backed Flowerpecker, Singapore

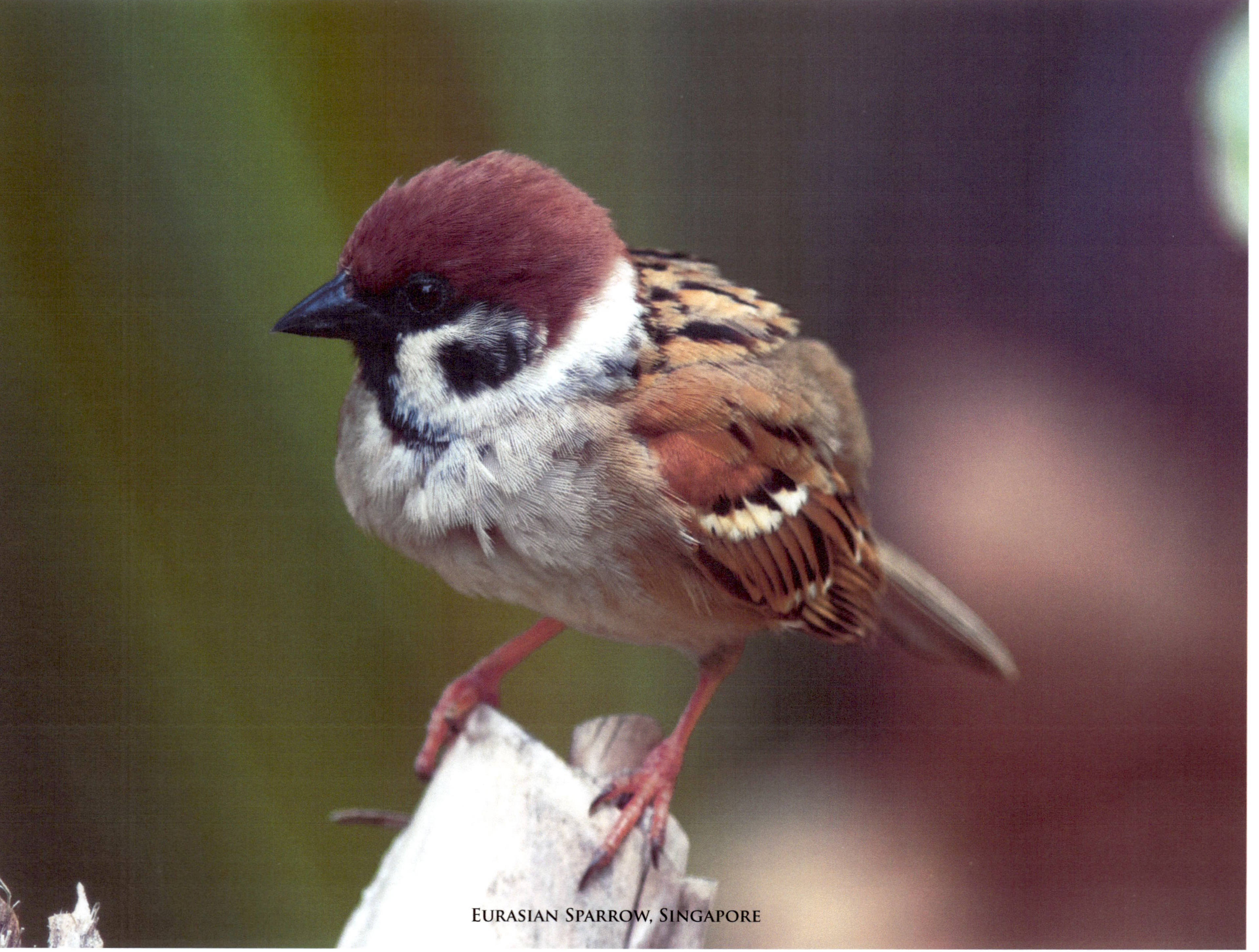

Eurasian Sparrow, Singapore

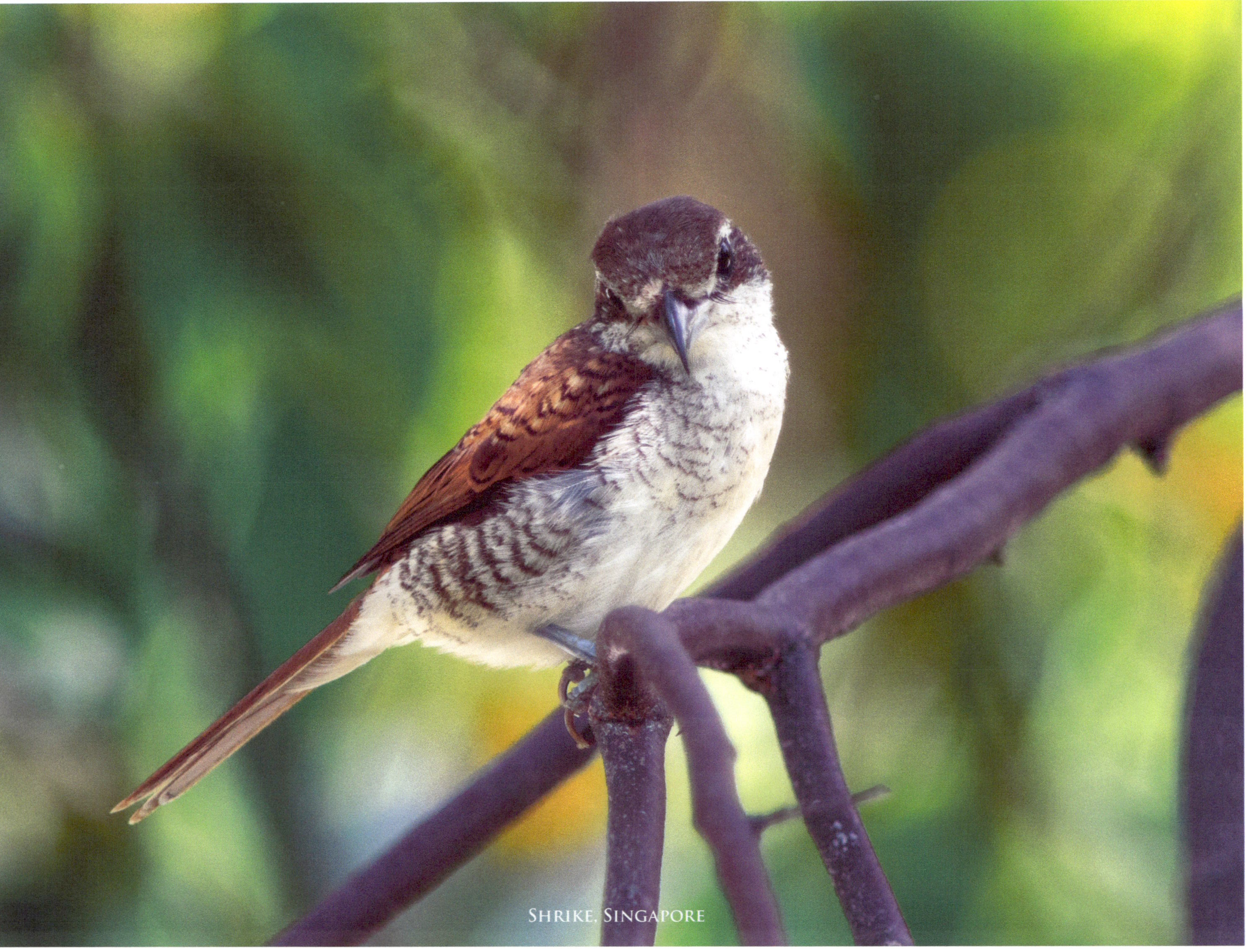
Shrike, Singapore

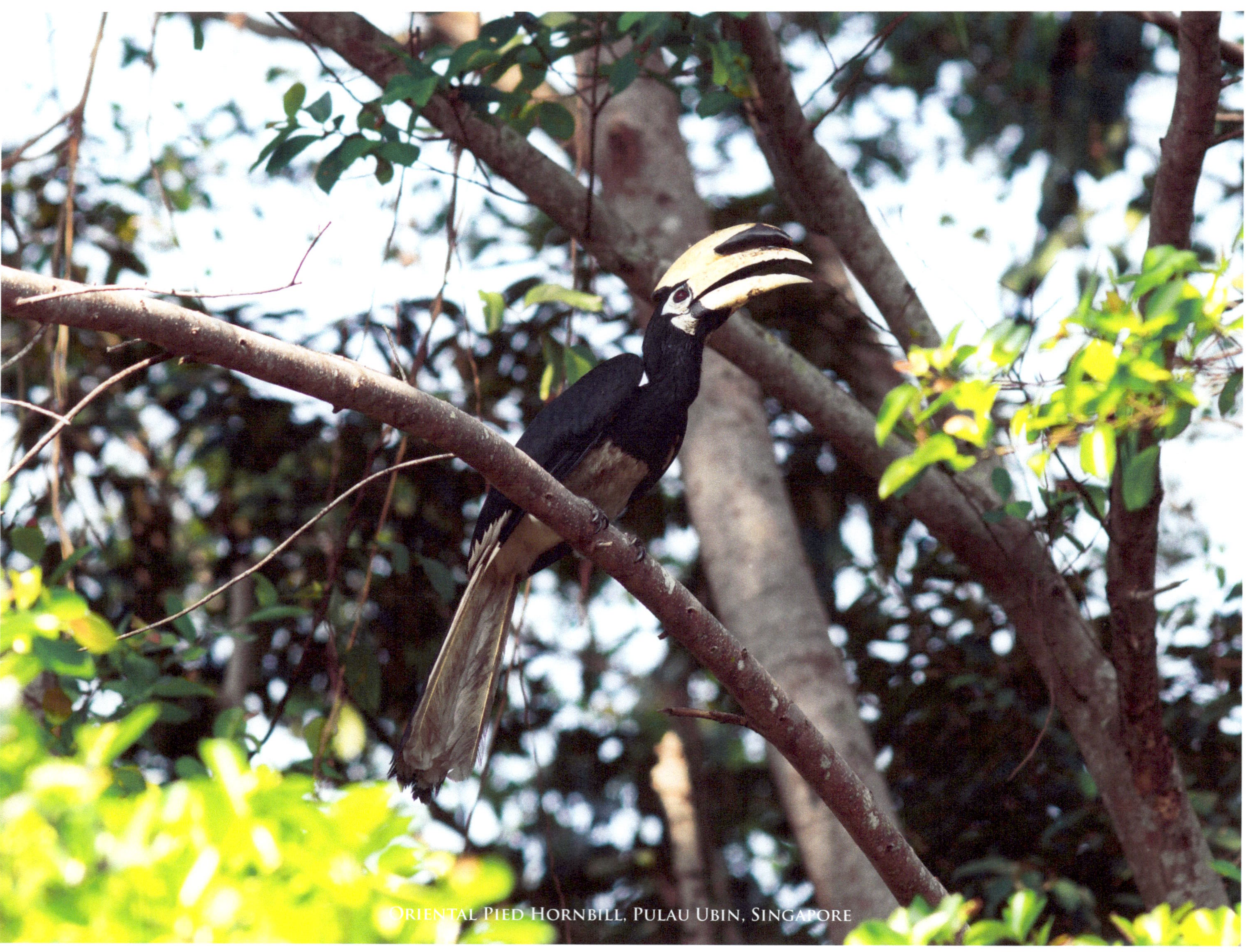

Oriental Pied Hornbill, Pulau Ubin, Singapore

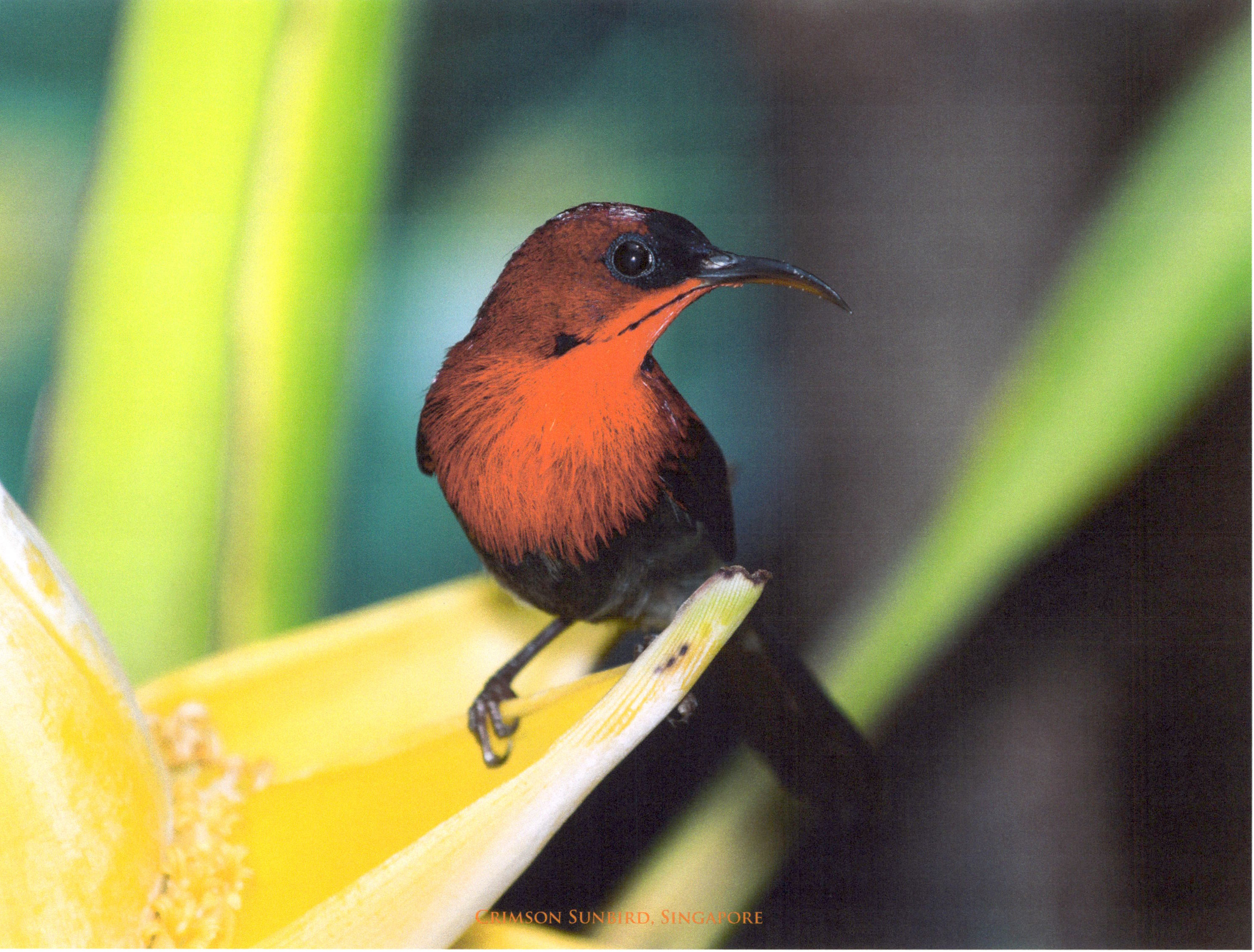

Crimson Sunbird, Singapore

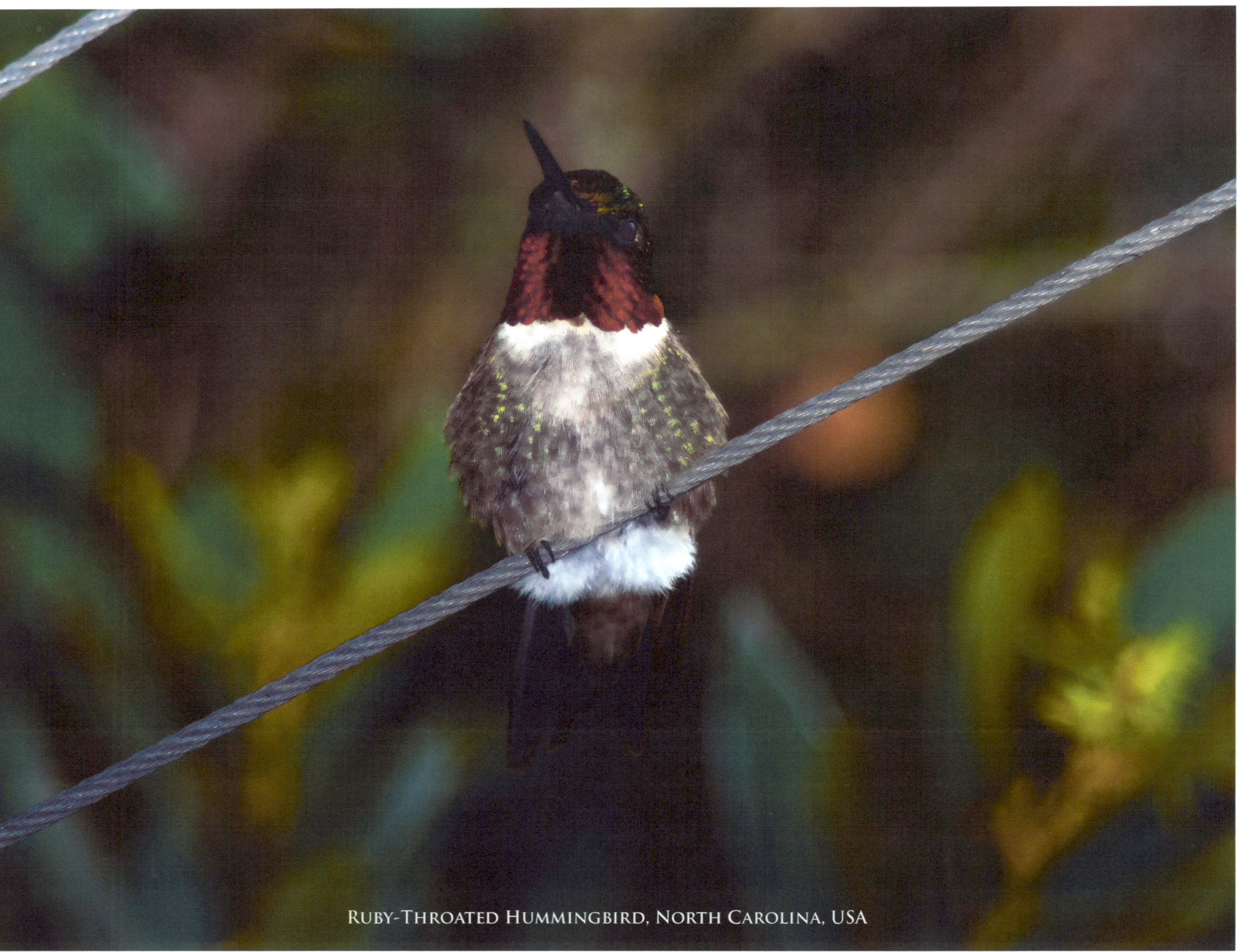

Ruby-Throated Hummingbird, North Carolina, USA

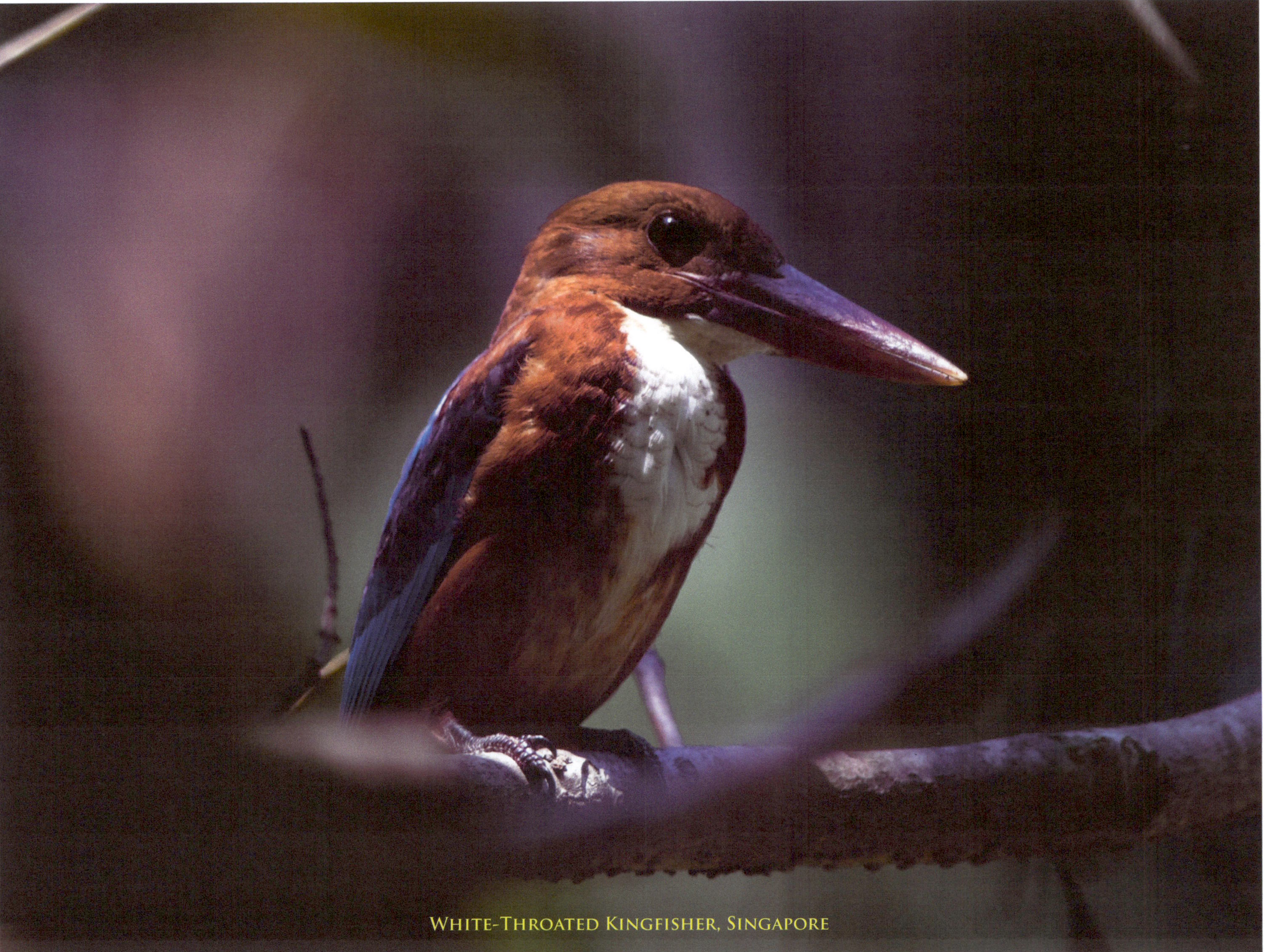

White-Throated Kingfisher, Singapore

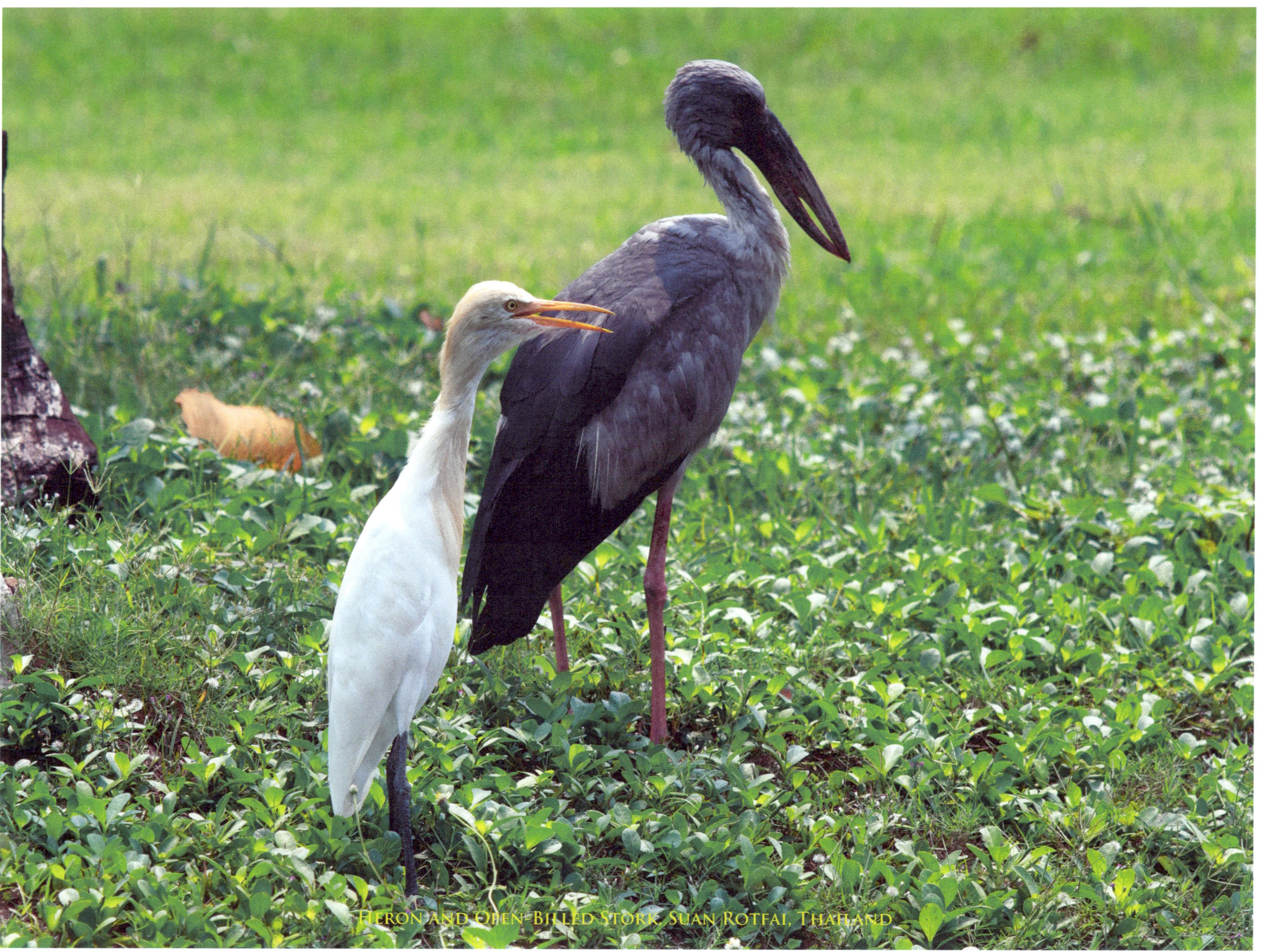

Heron and Open-Billed Stork, Suan Rotfai, Thailand

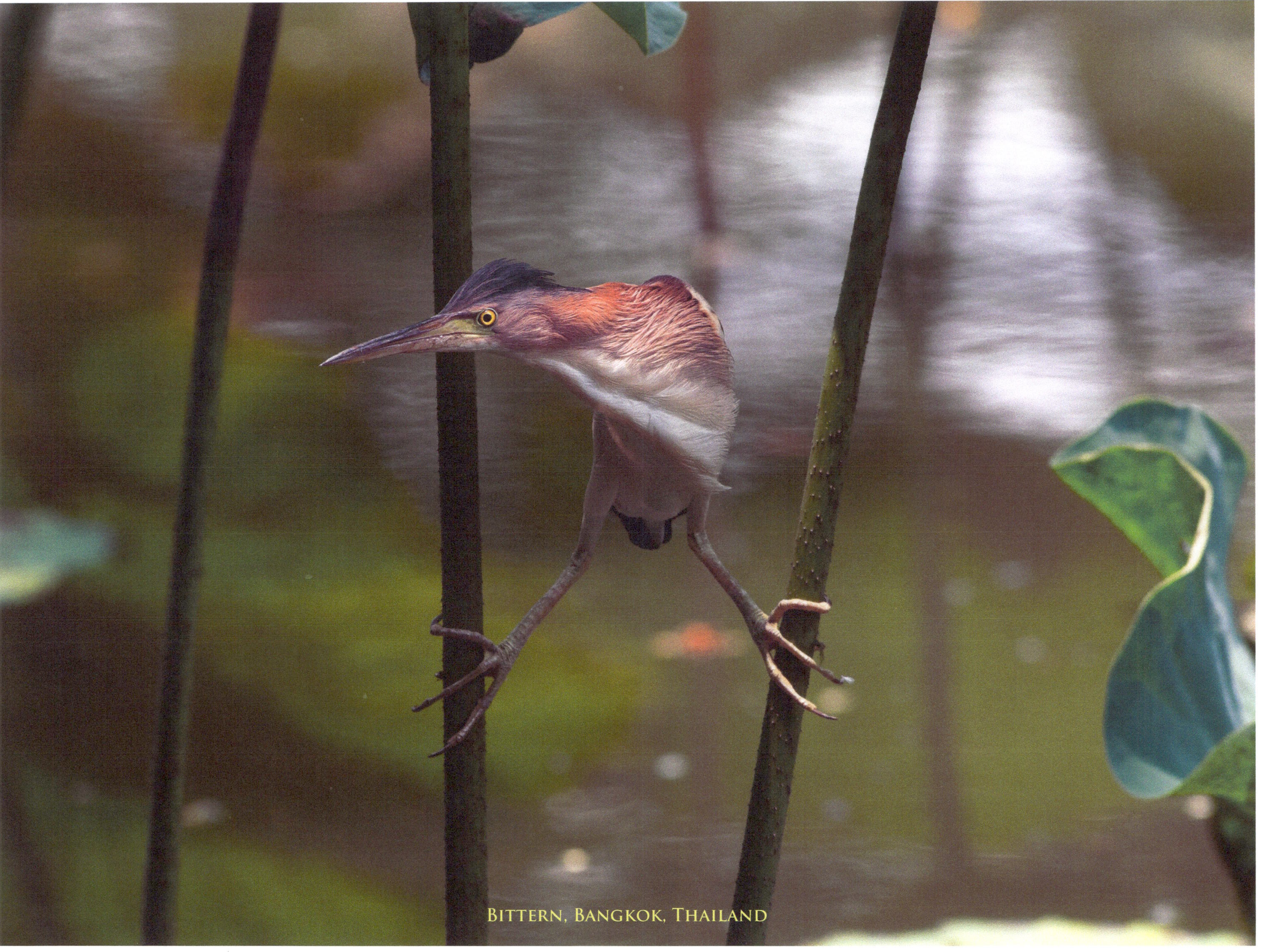

Bittern, Bangkok, Thailand

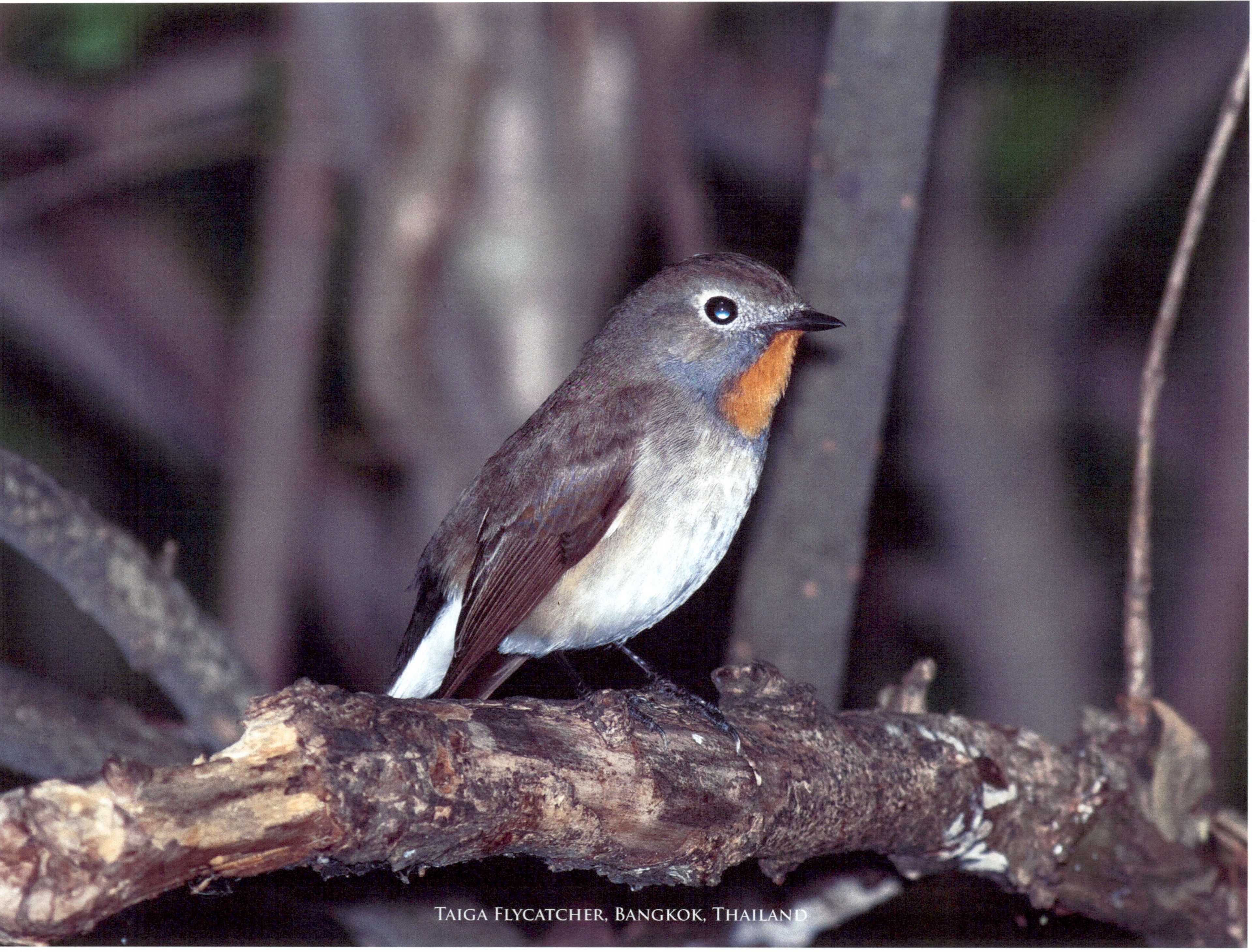

Taiga Flycatcher, Bangkok, Thailand

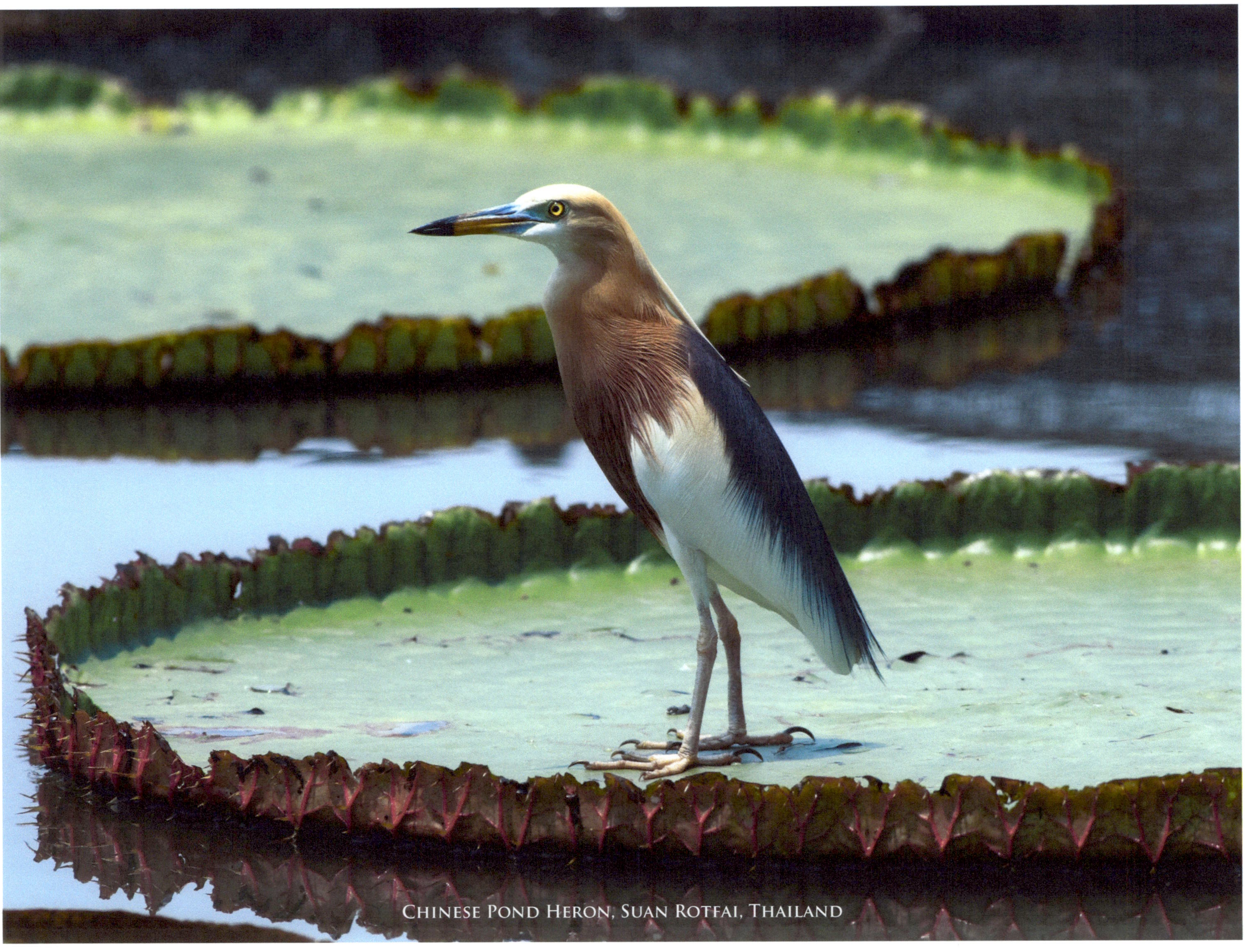

Chinese Pond Heron, Suan Rotfai, Thailand

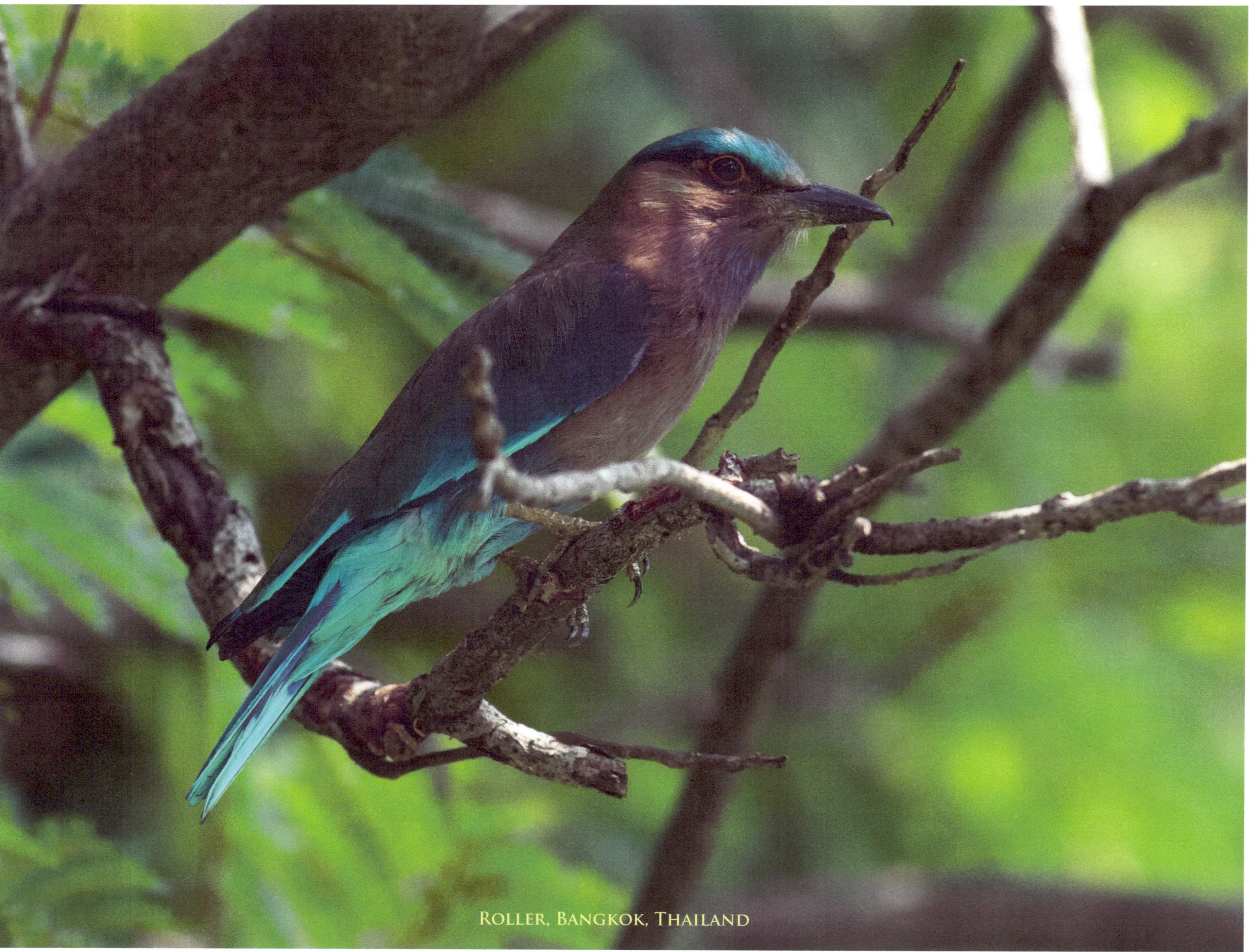

Roller, Bangkok, Thailand

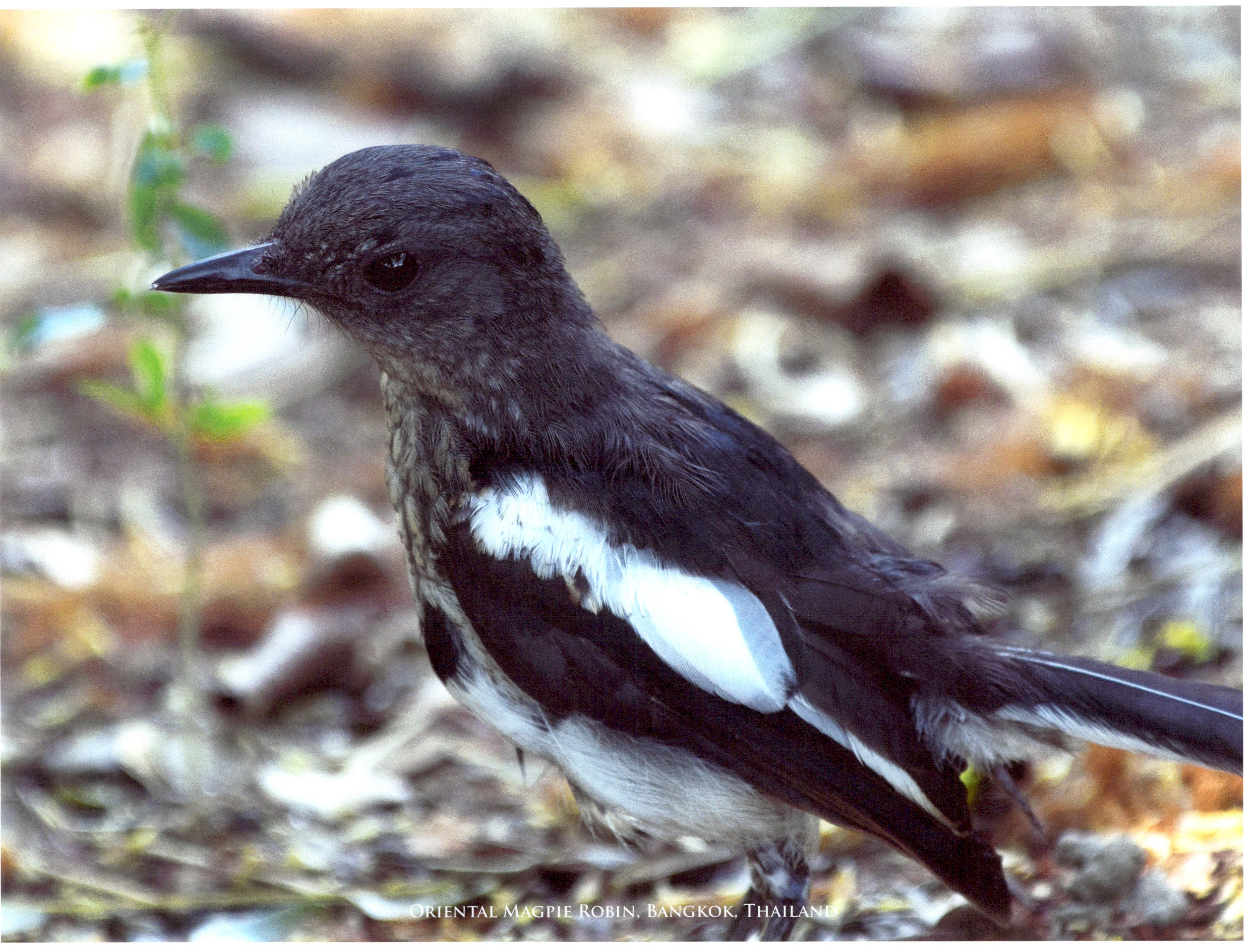

Oriental Magpie Robin, Bangkok, Thailand

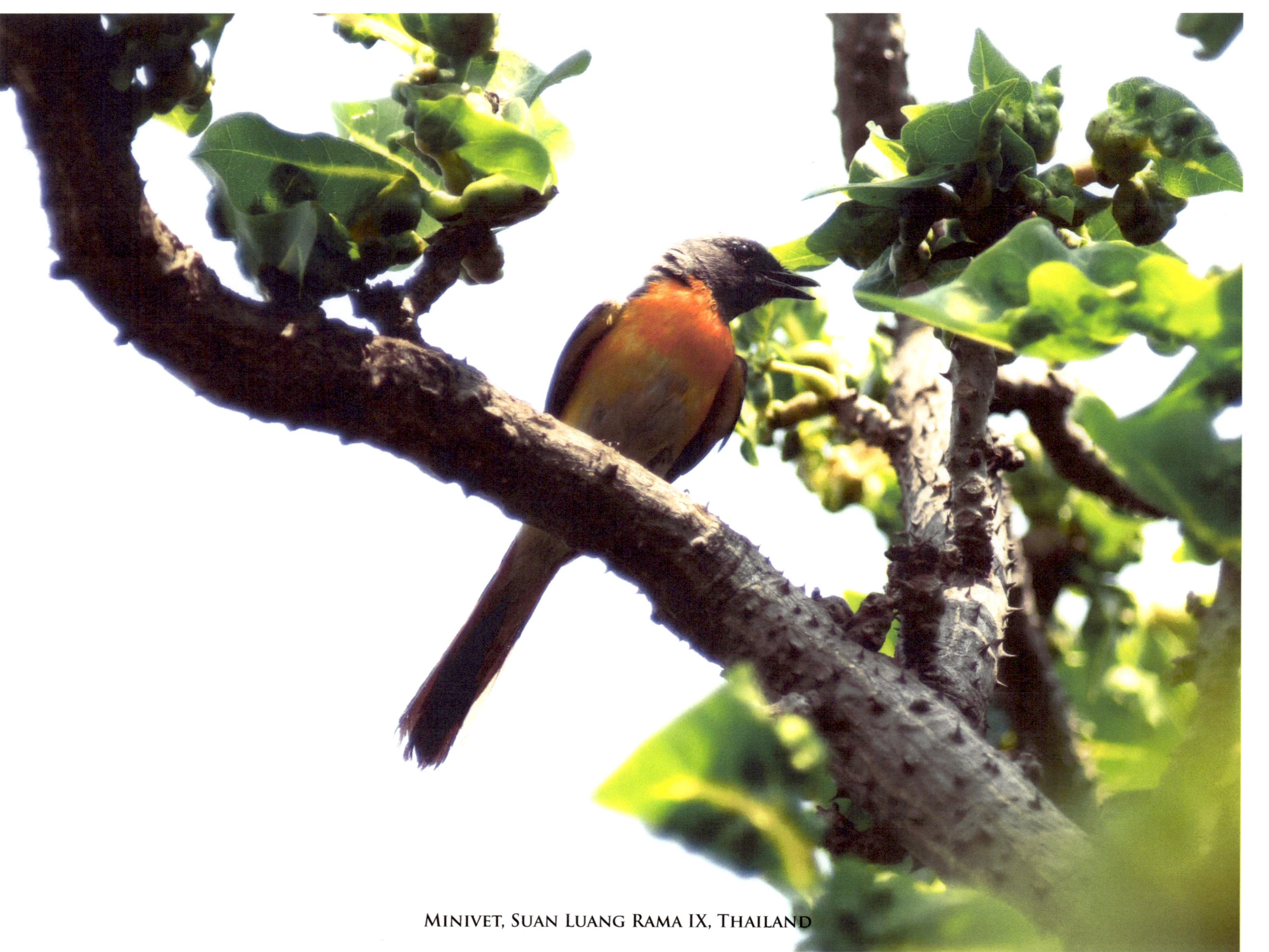

Minivet, Suan Luang Rama IX, Thailand

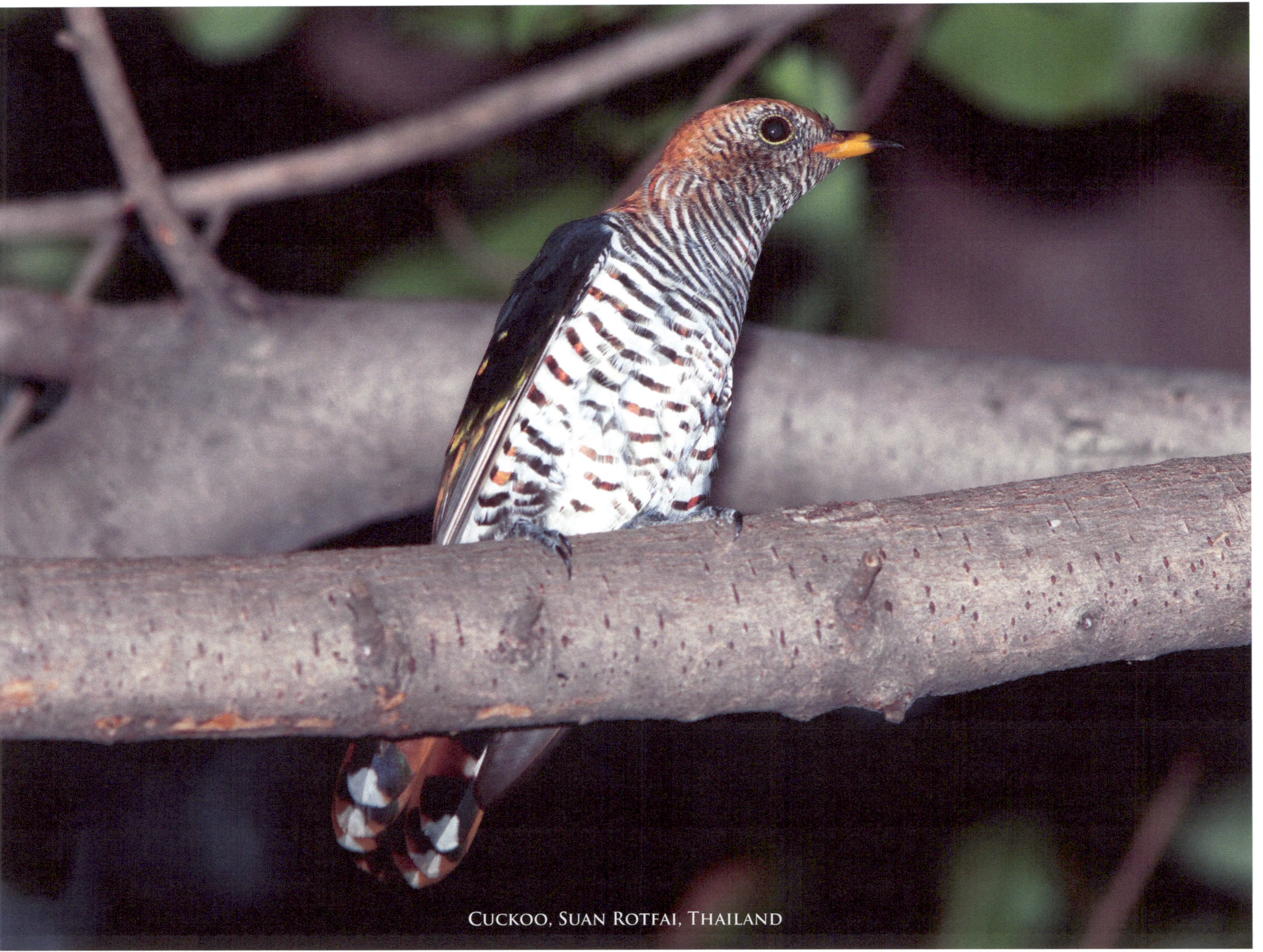

Cuckoo, Suan Rotfai, Thailand

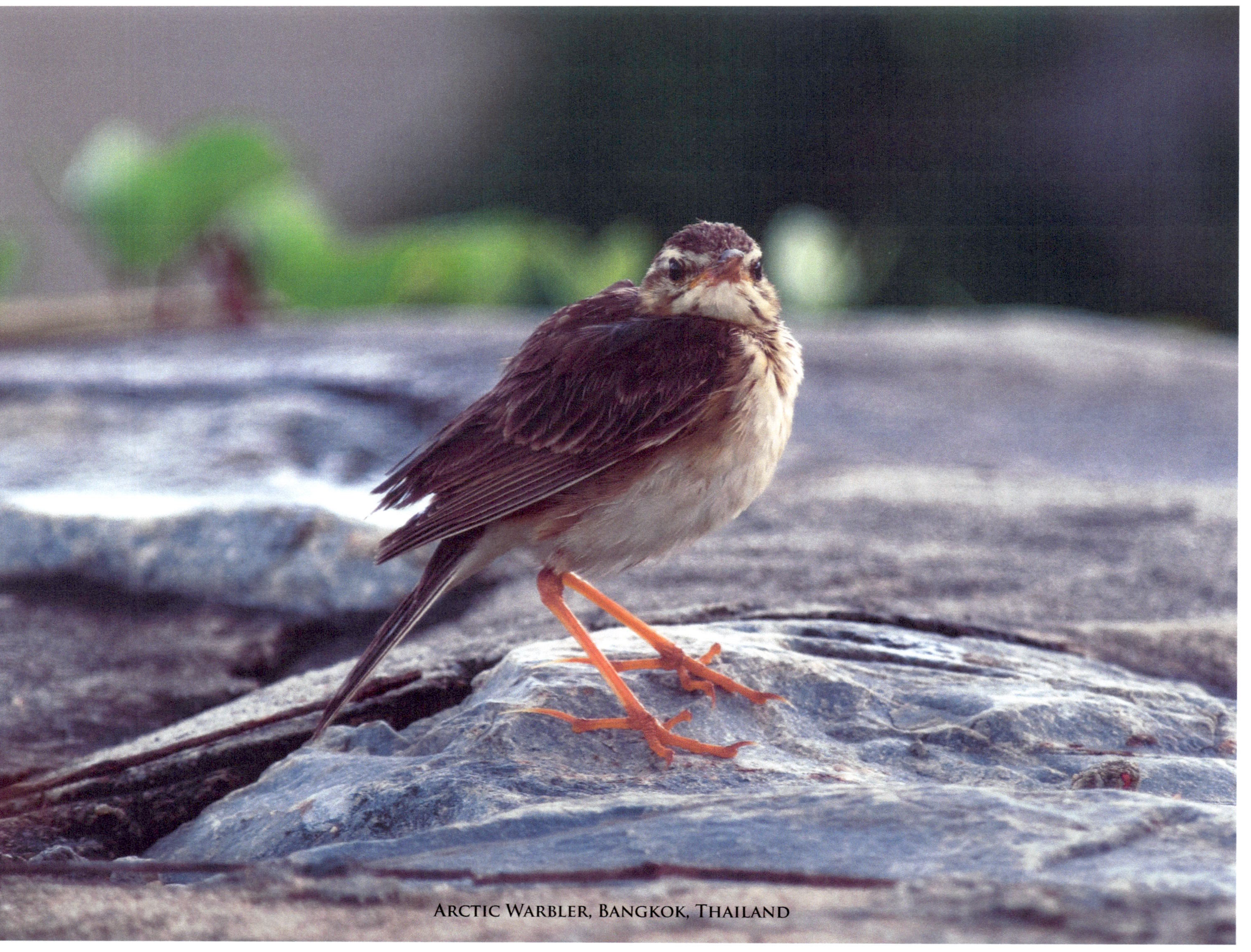

Arctic Warbler, Bangkok, Thailand

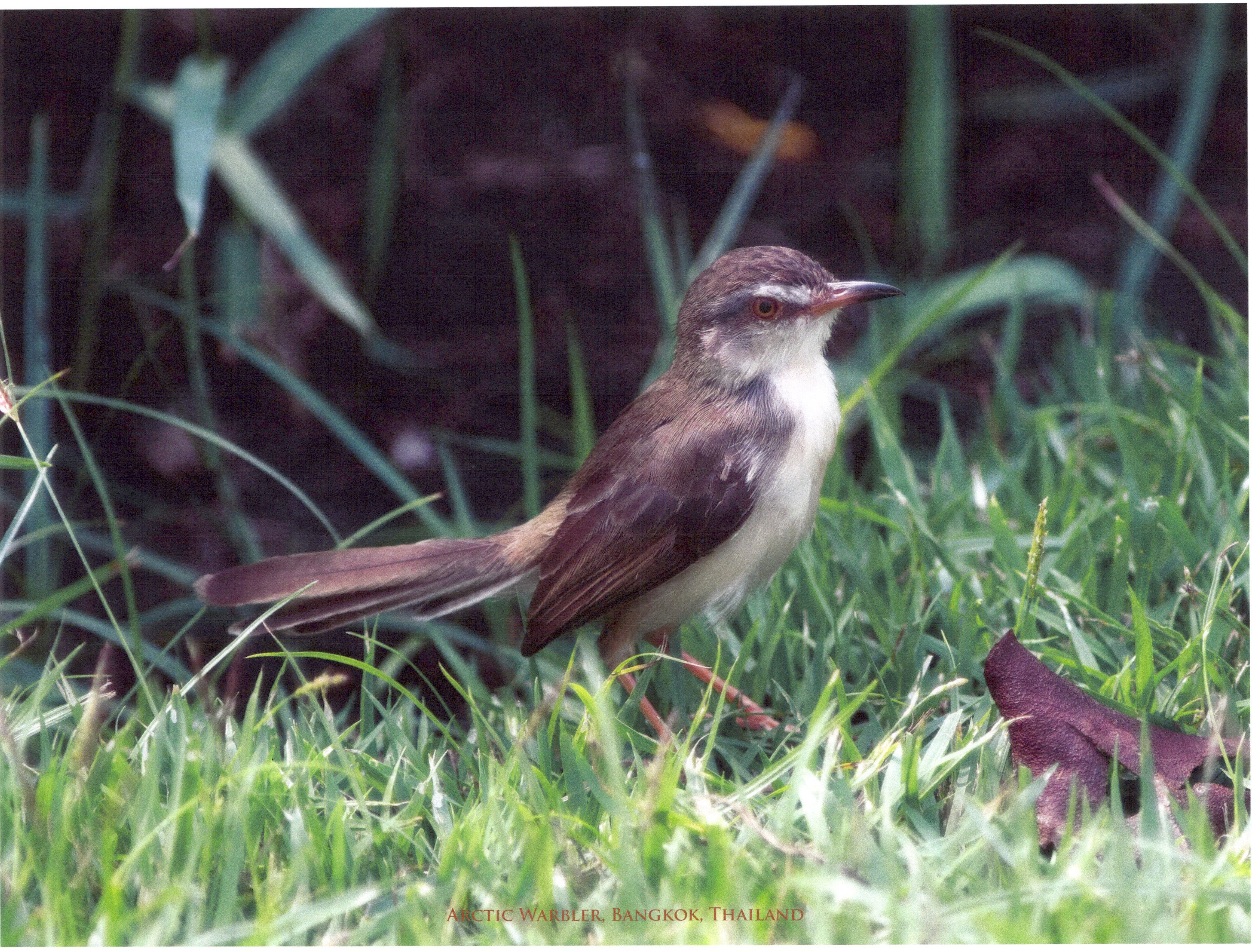

Arctic Warbler, Bangkok, Thailand

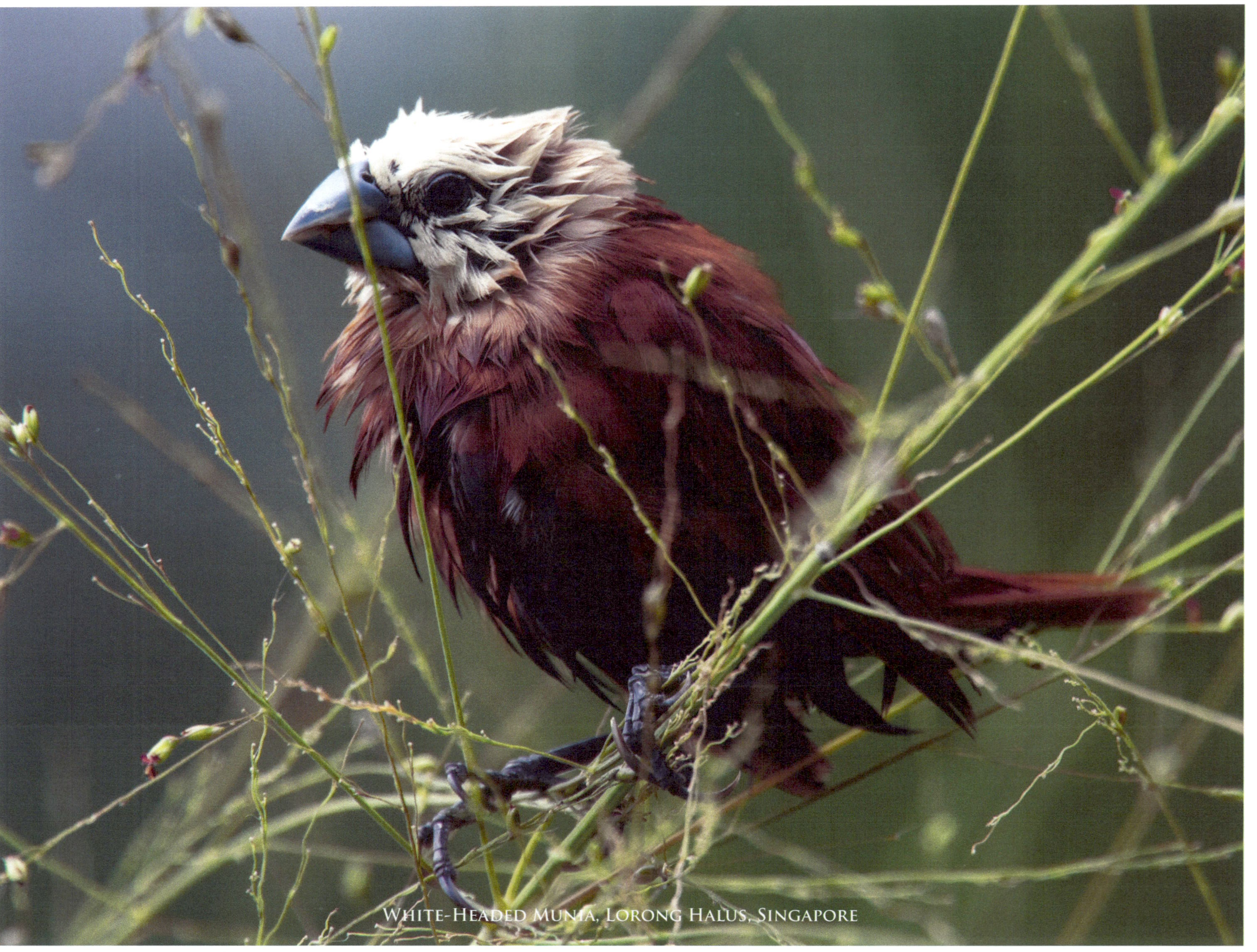

White-Headed Munia, Lorong Halus, Singapore

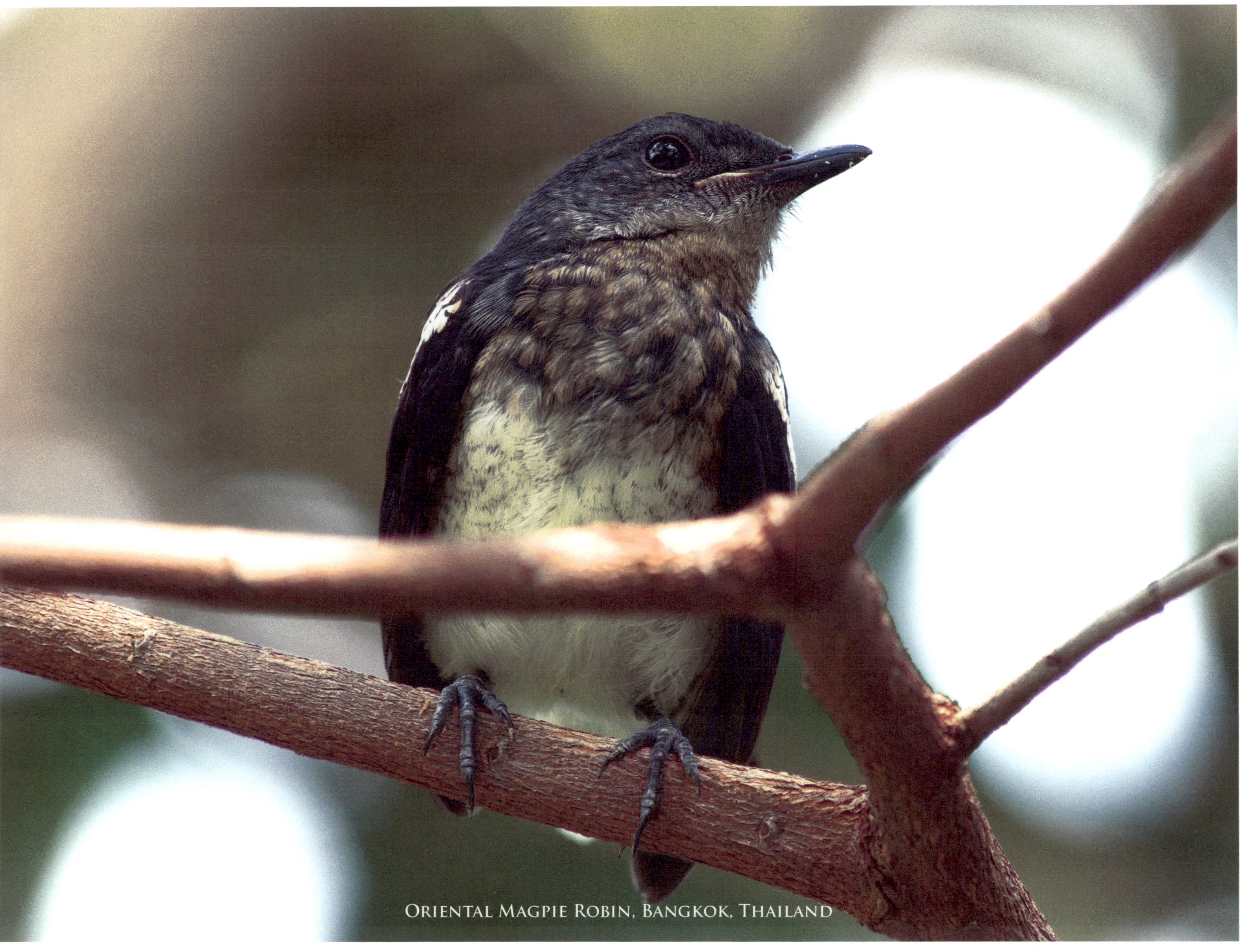

Oriental Magpie Robin, Bangkok, Thailand

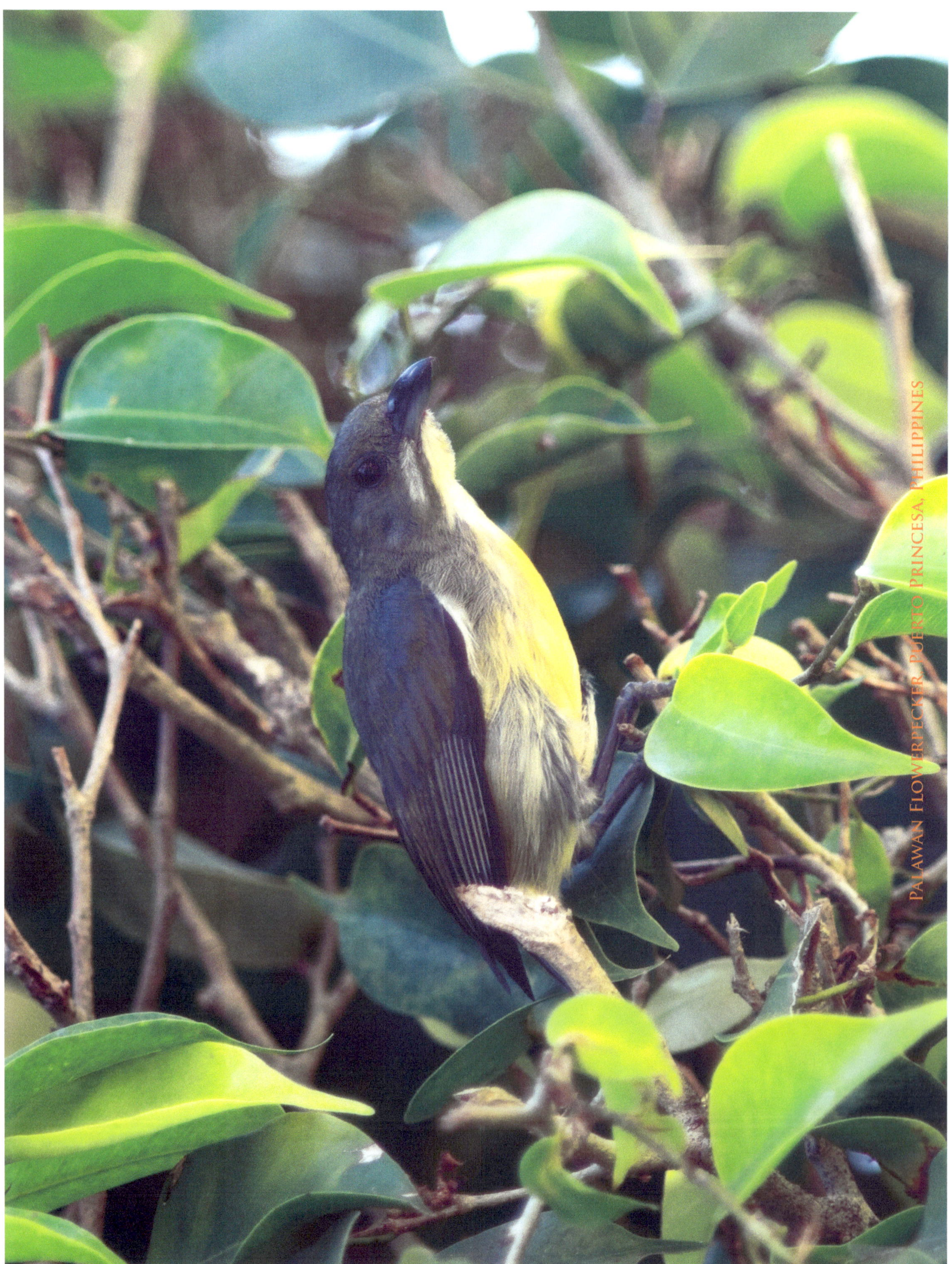

Palawan Flowerpecker, Puerto Princesa, Philippines

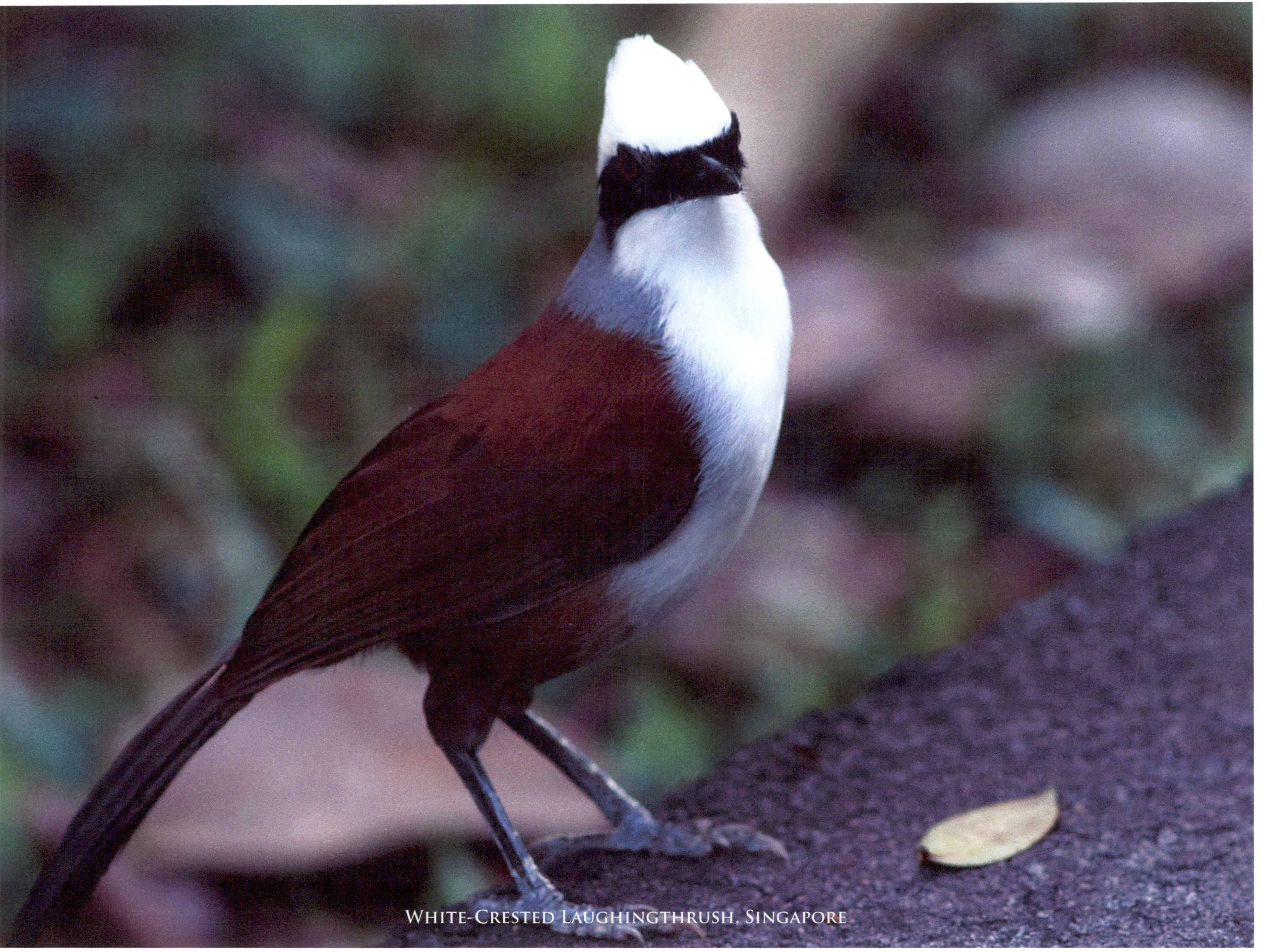

White-Crested Laughingthrush, Singapore

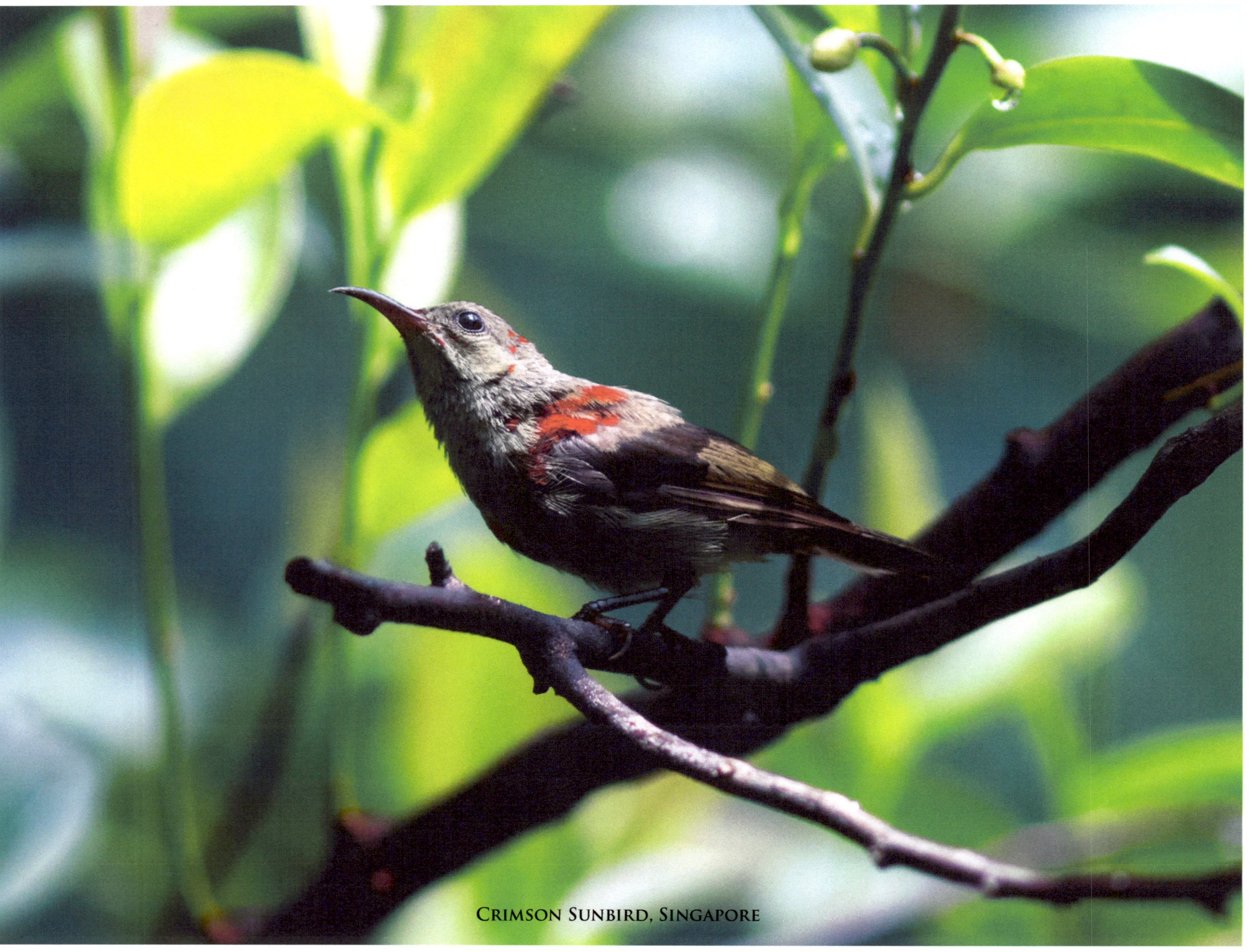

Crimson Sunbird, Singapore

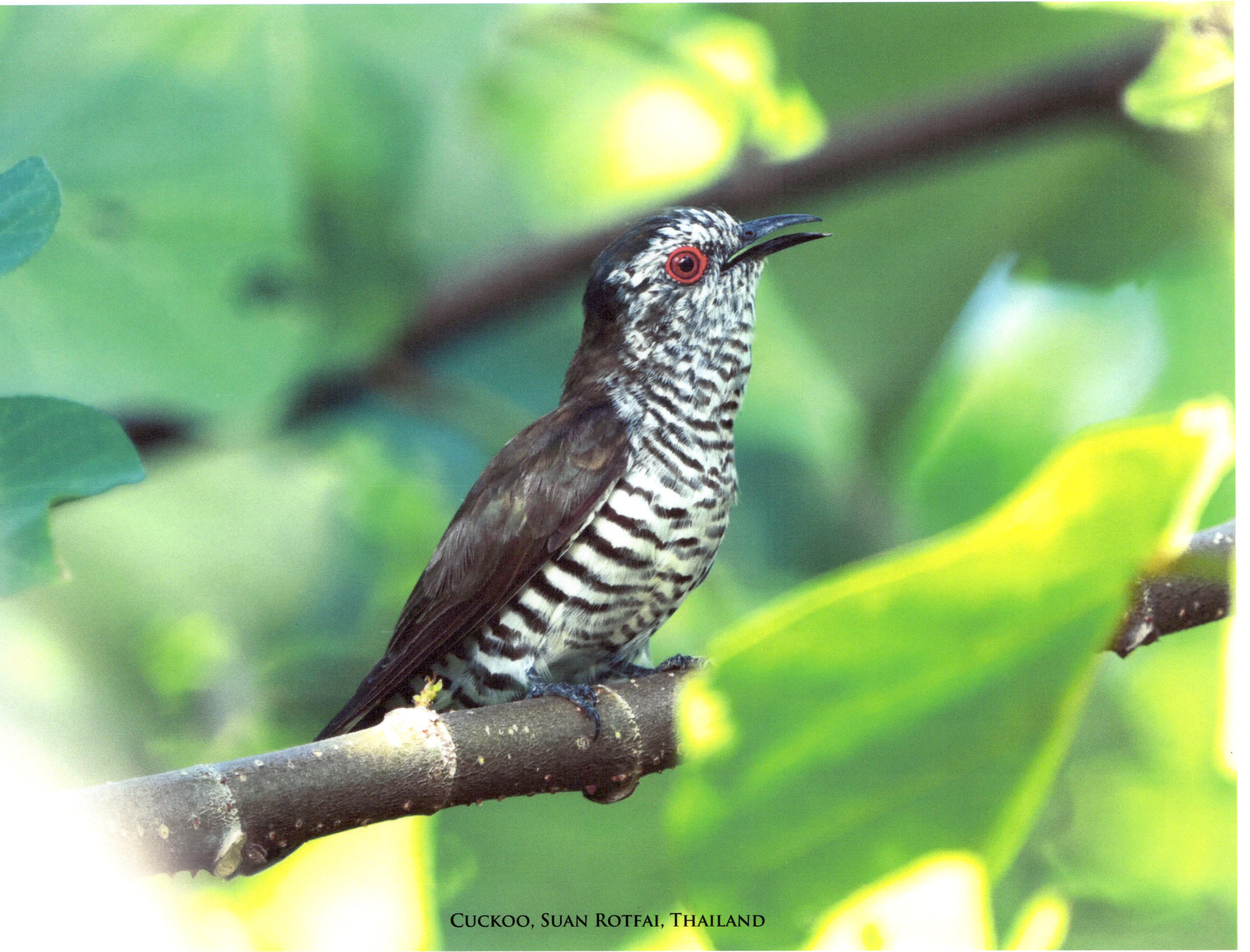

Cuckoo, Suan Rotfai, Thailand

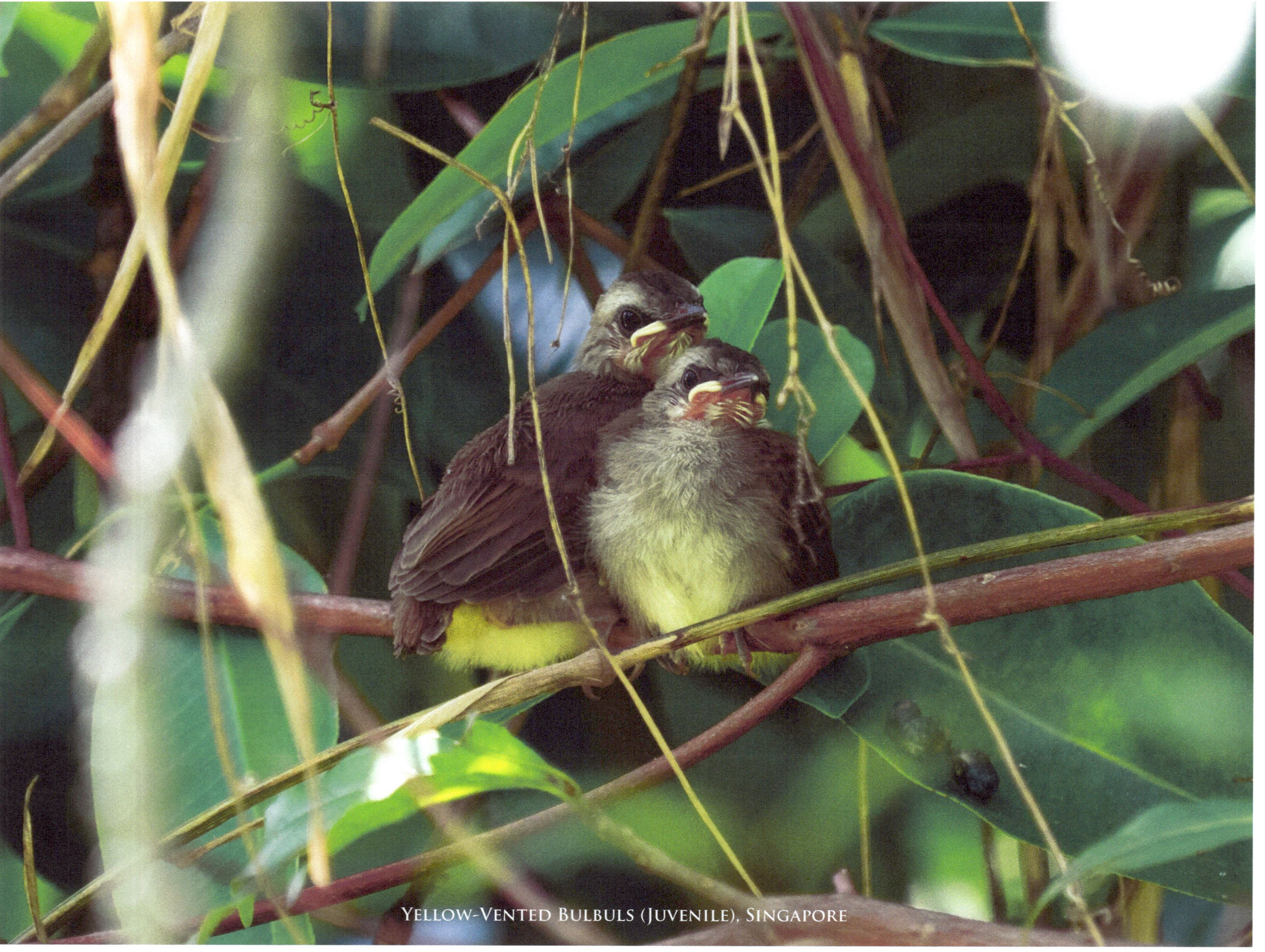

Yellow-Vented Bulbuls (Juvenile), Singapore

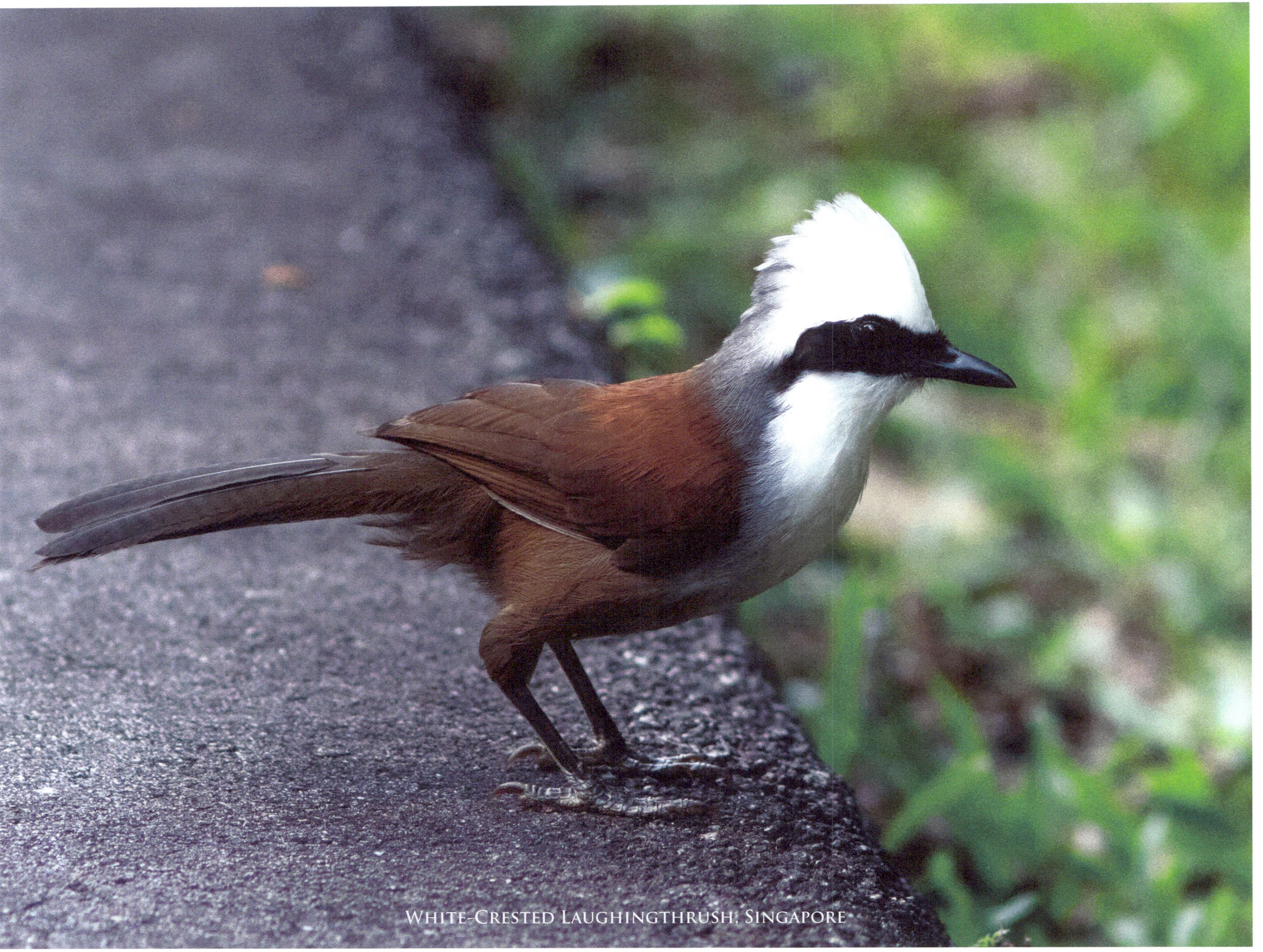

White-Crested Laughingthrush, Singapore

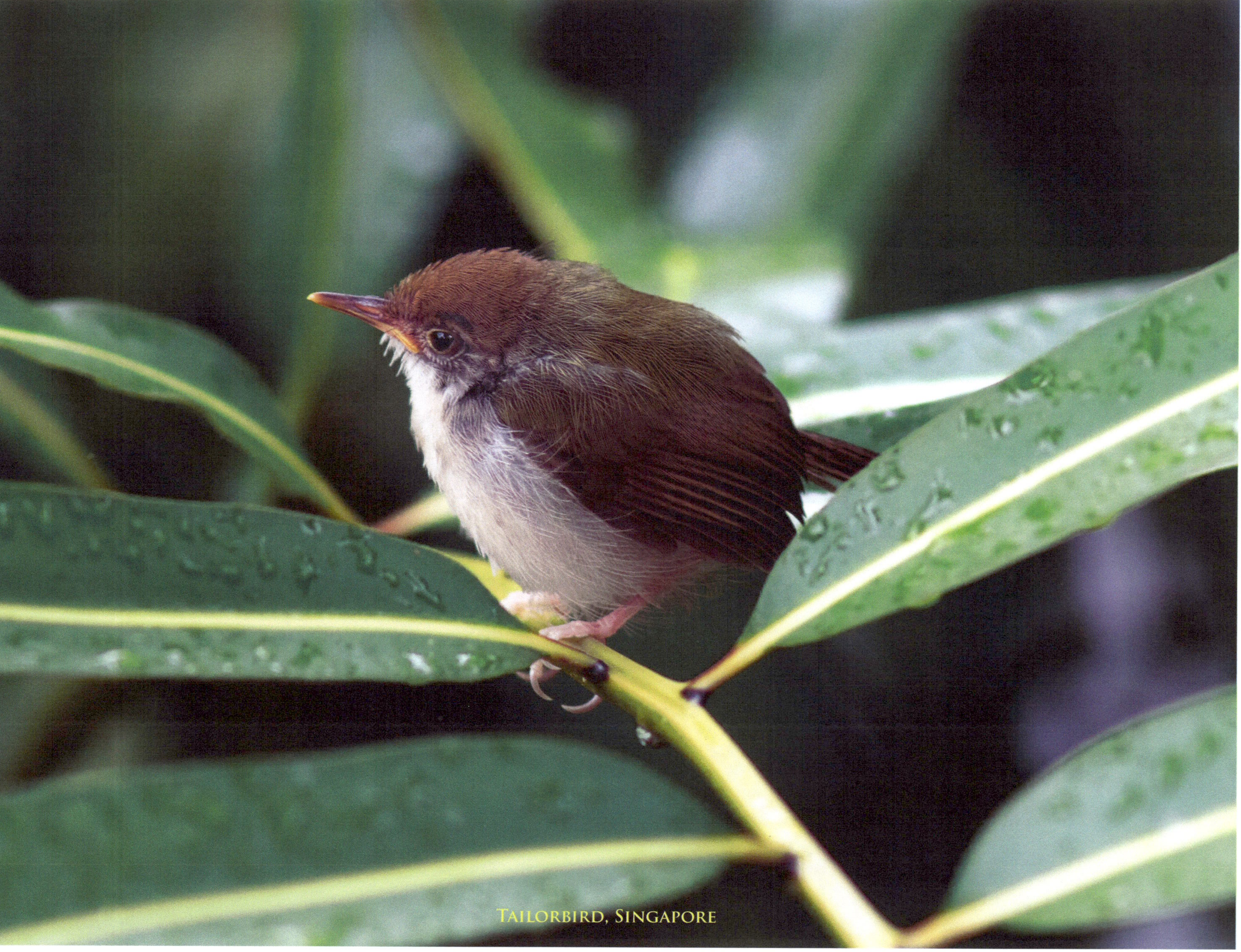

Tailorbird, Singapore

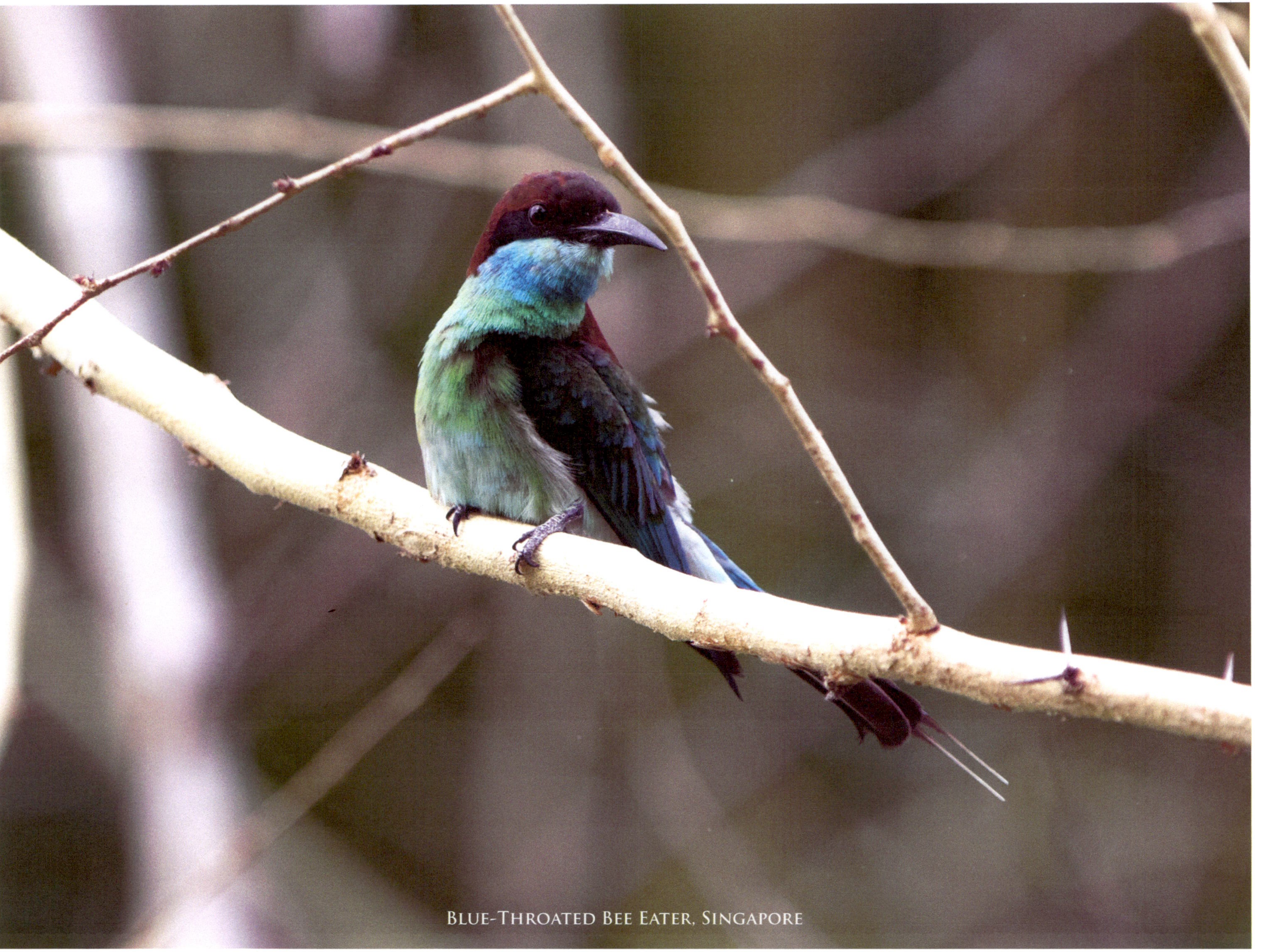

Blue-Throated Bee Eater, Singapore

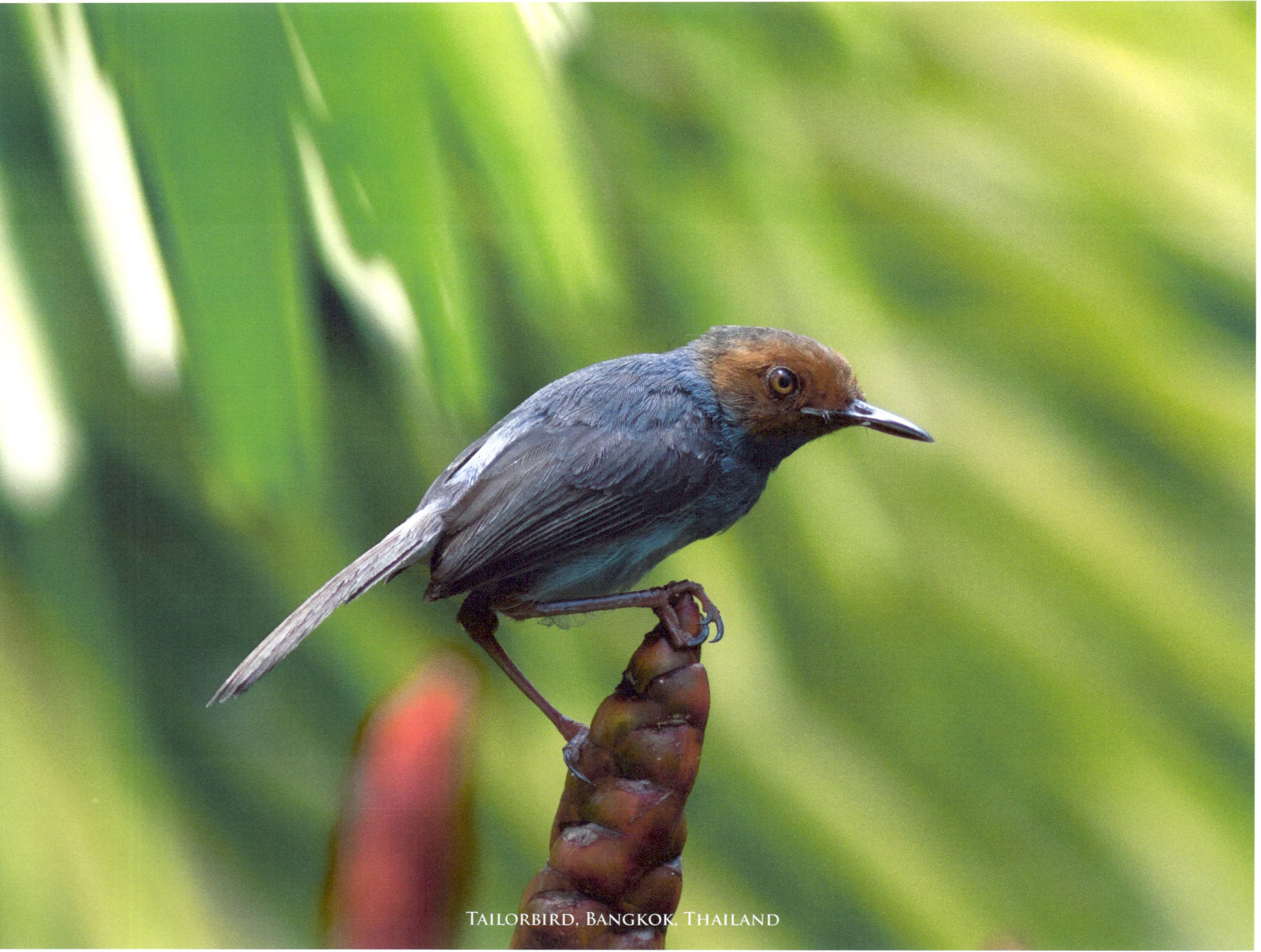

Tailorbird, Bangkok, Thailand

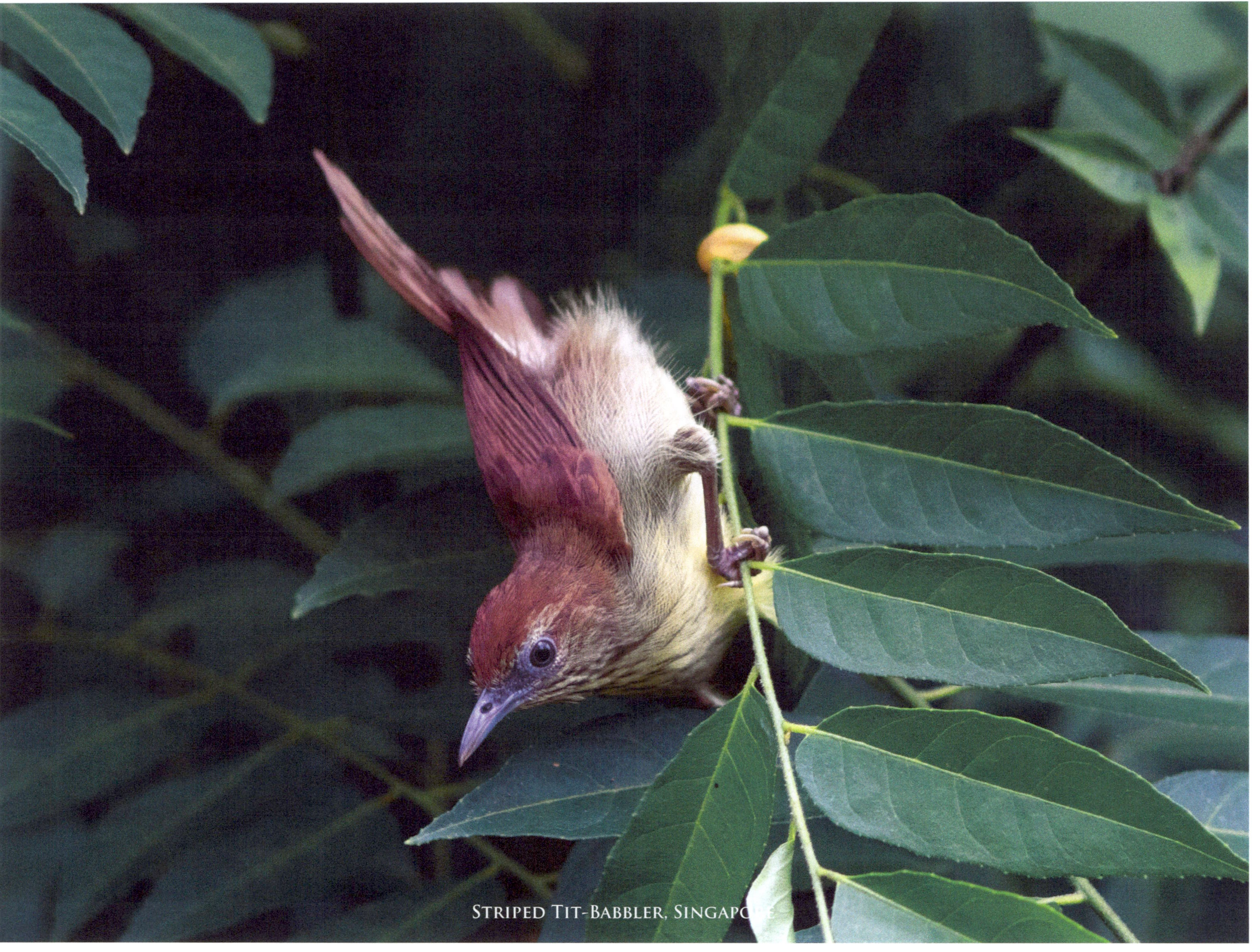

Striped Tit-Babbler, Singapore

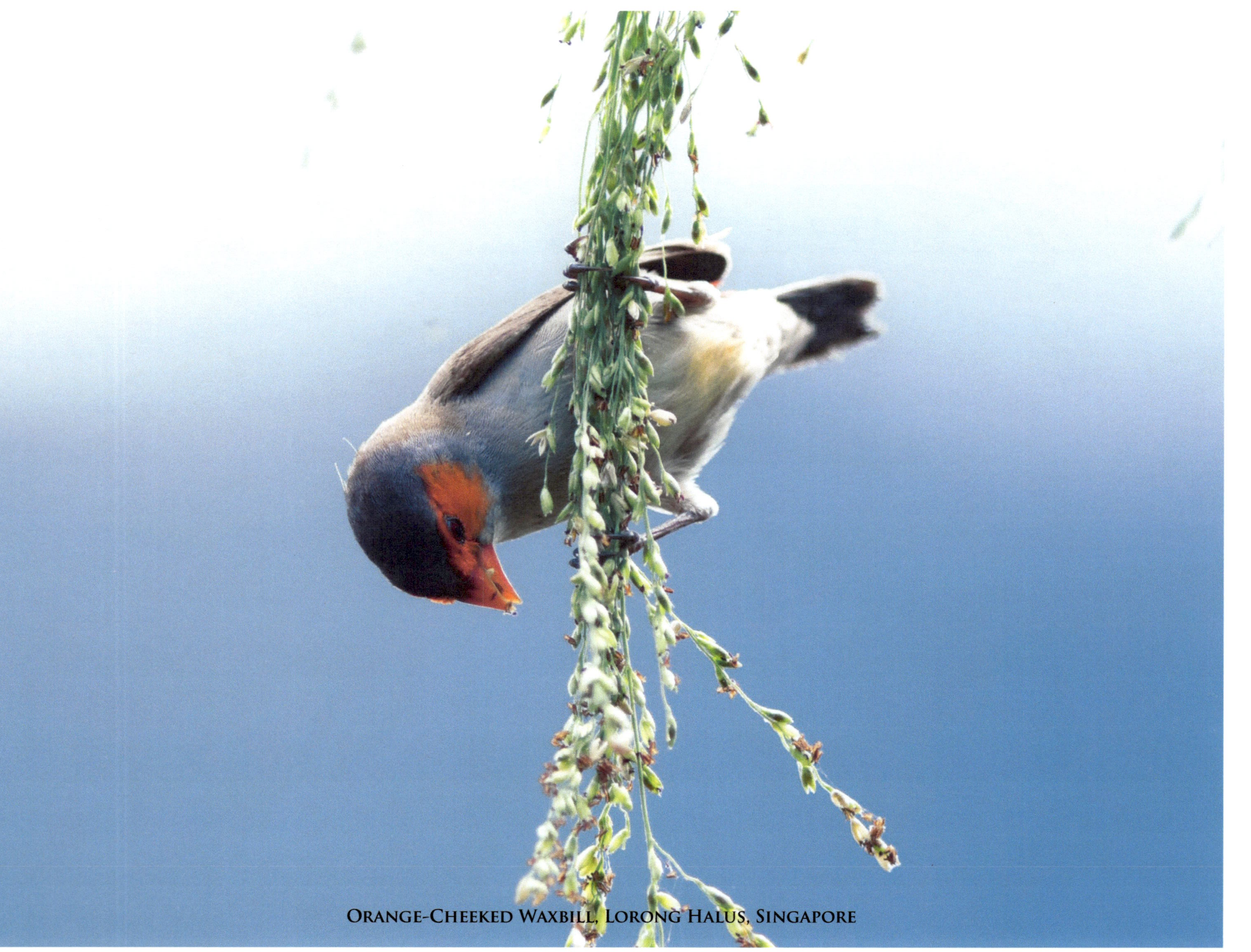

Orange-Cheeked Waxbill, Lorong Halus, Singapore

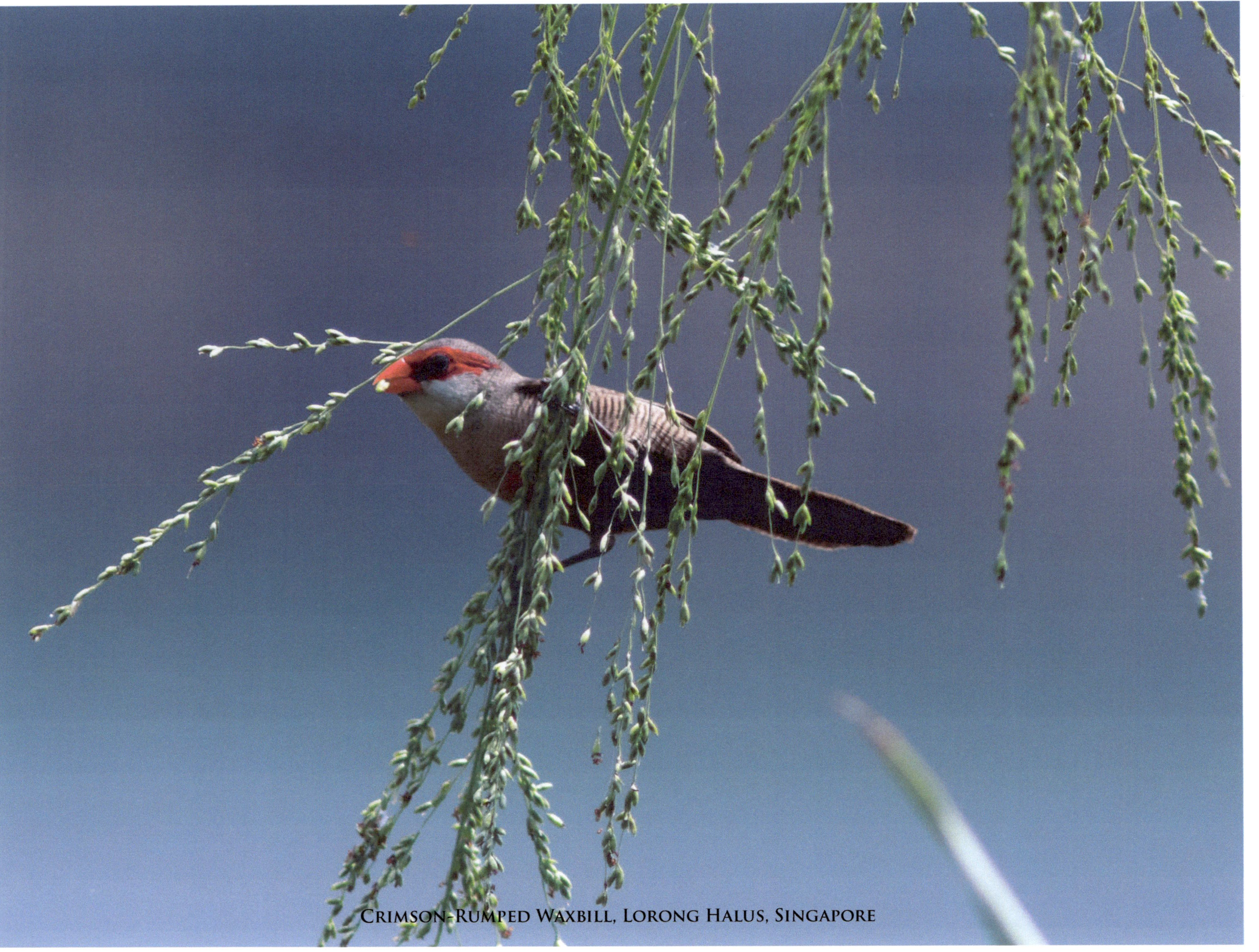

Crimson-Rumped Waxbill, Lorong Halus, Singapore

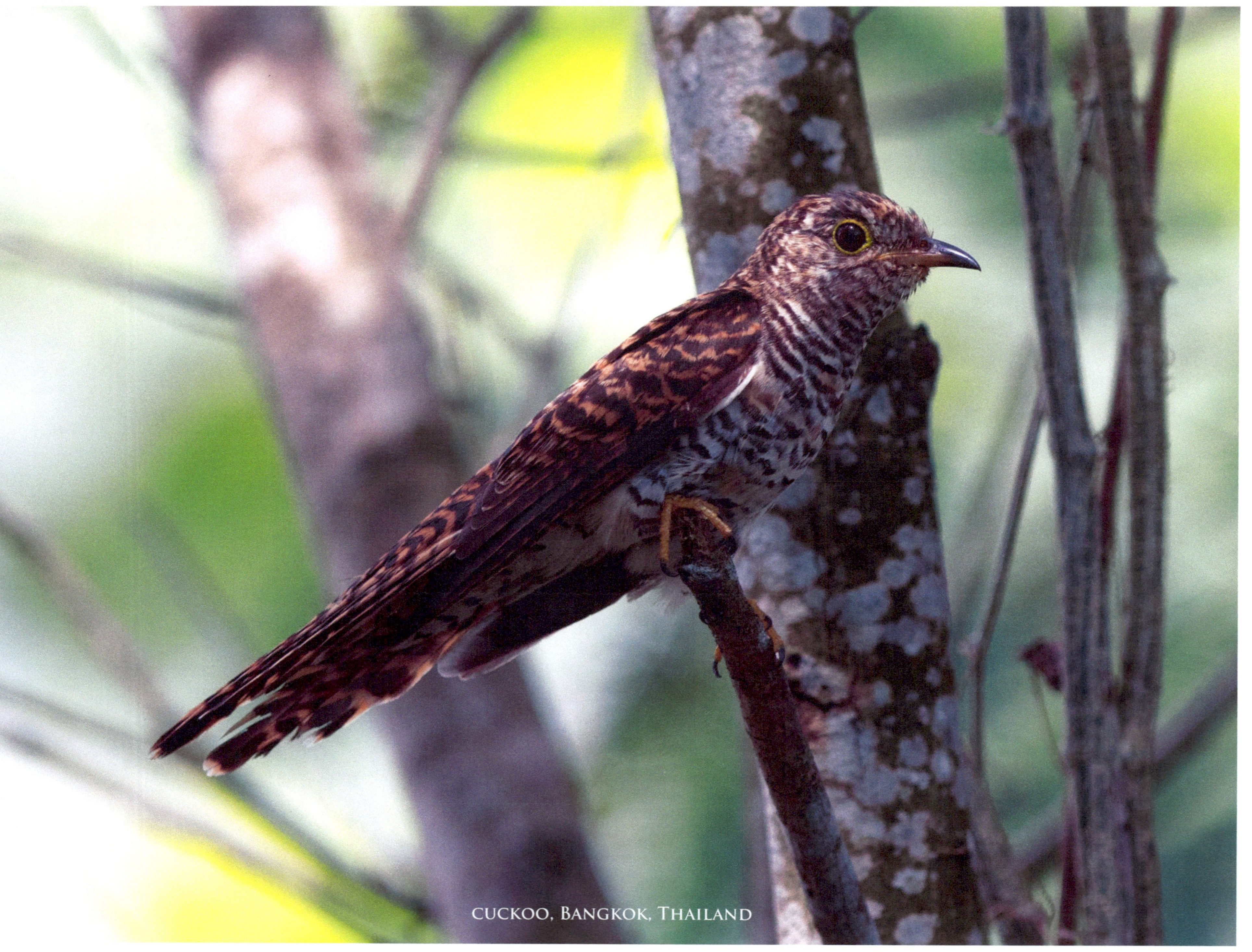

Cuckoo, Bangkok, Thailand

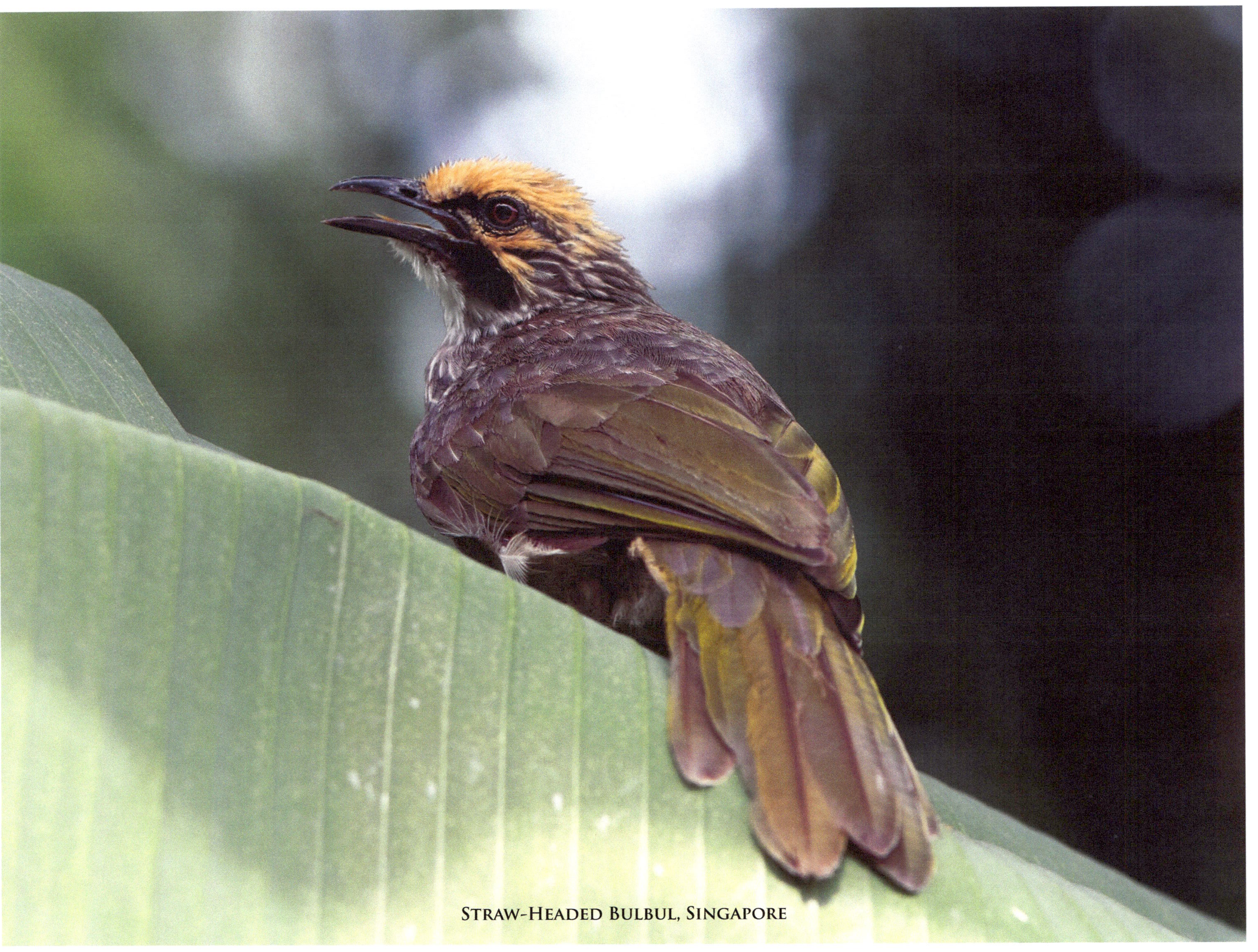

Straw-Headed Bulbul, Singapore

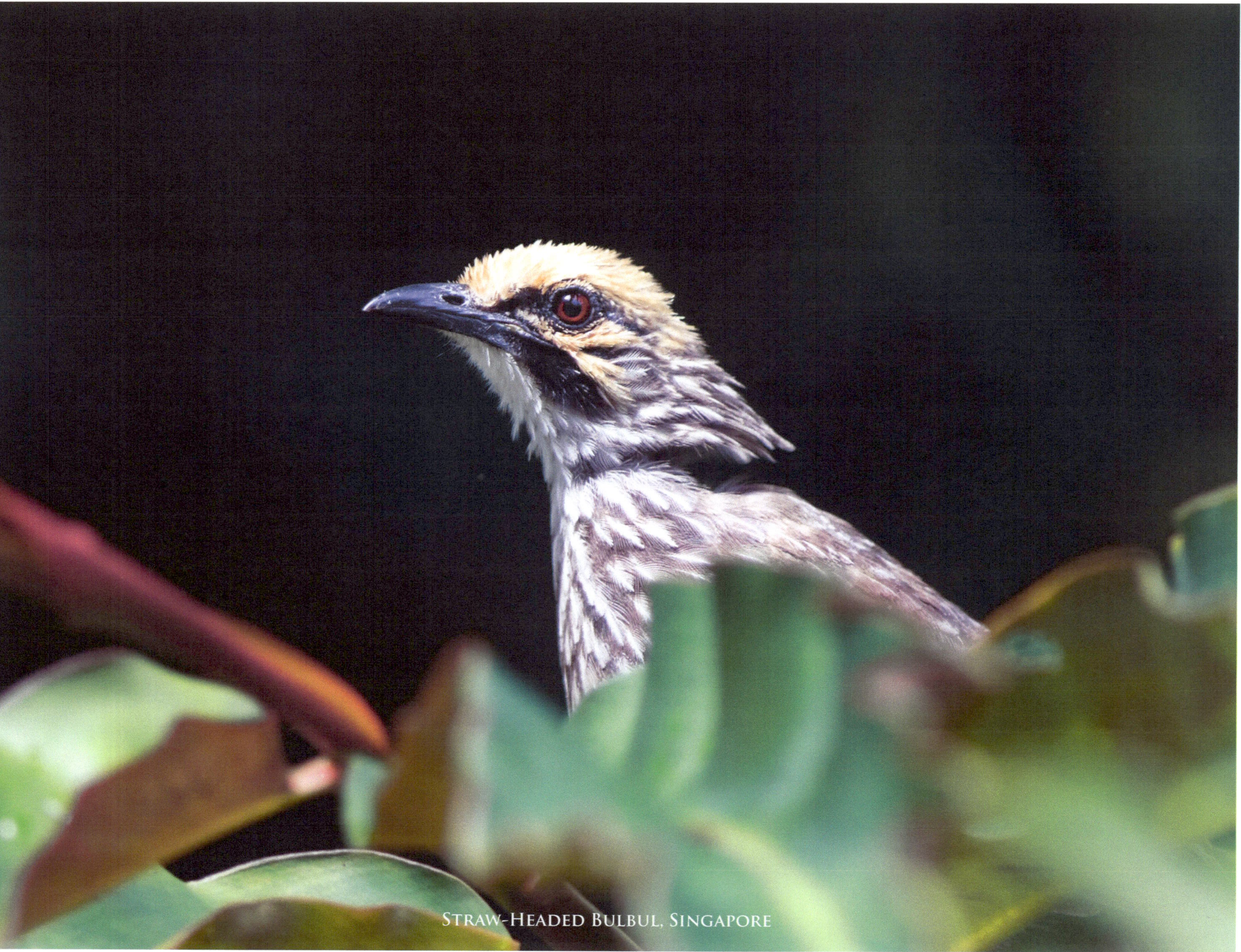

Straw-Headed Bulbul, Singapore

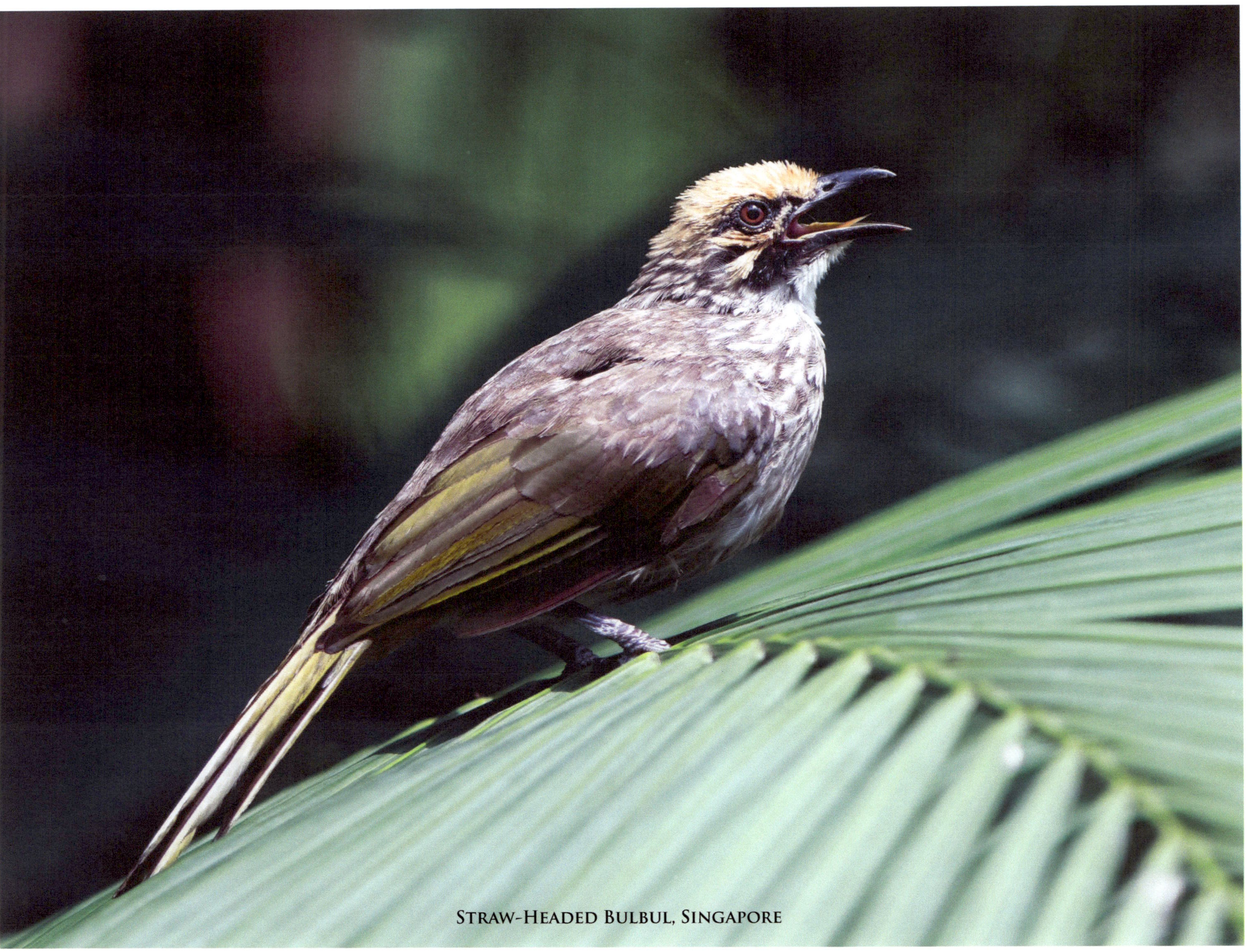

Straw-Headed Bulbul, Singapore

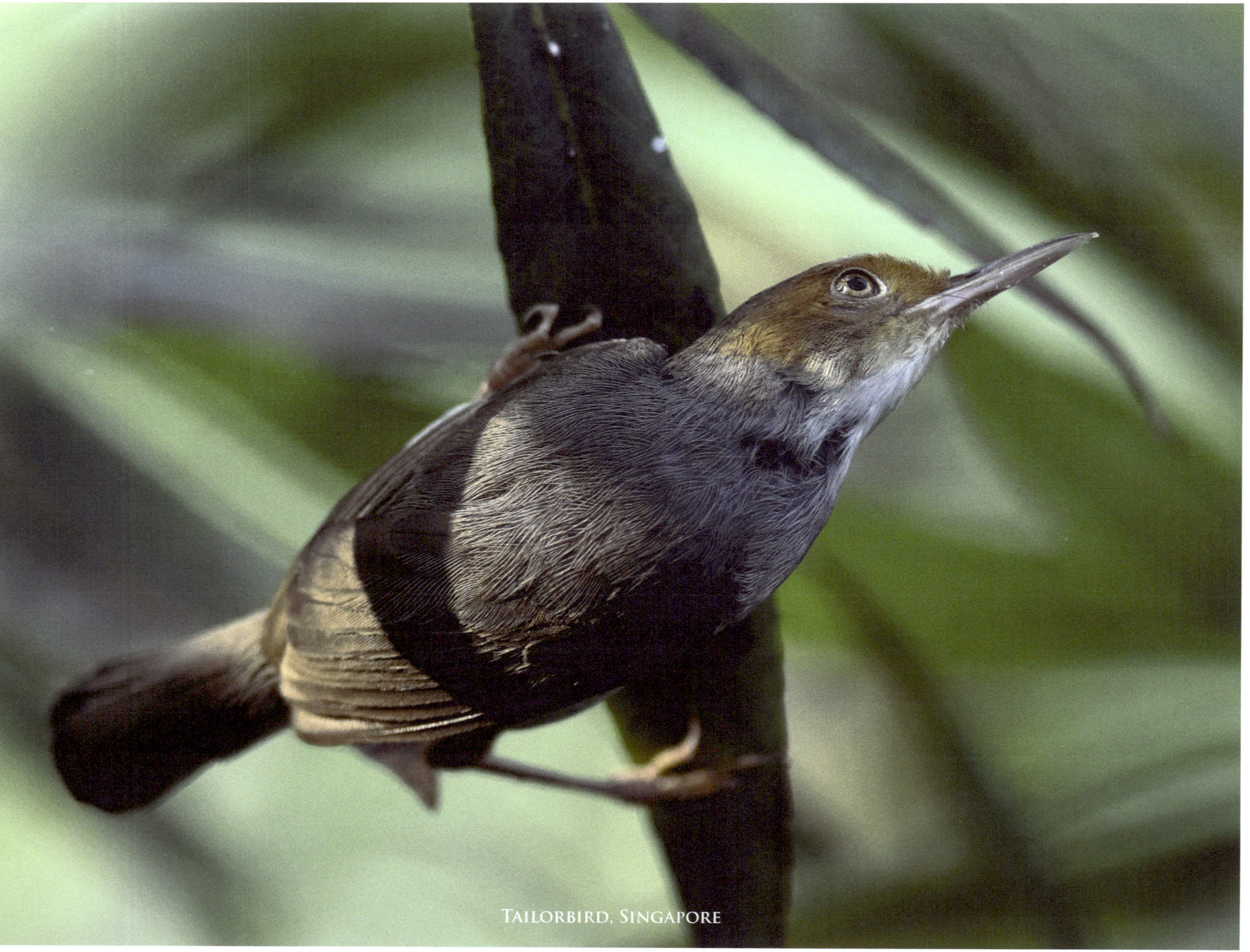

Tailorbird, Singapore

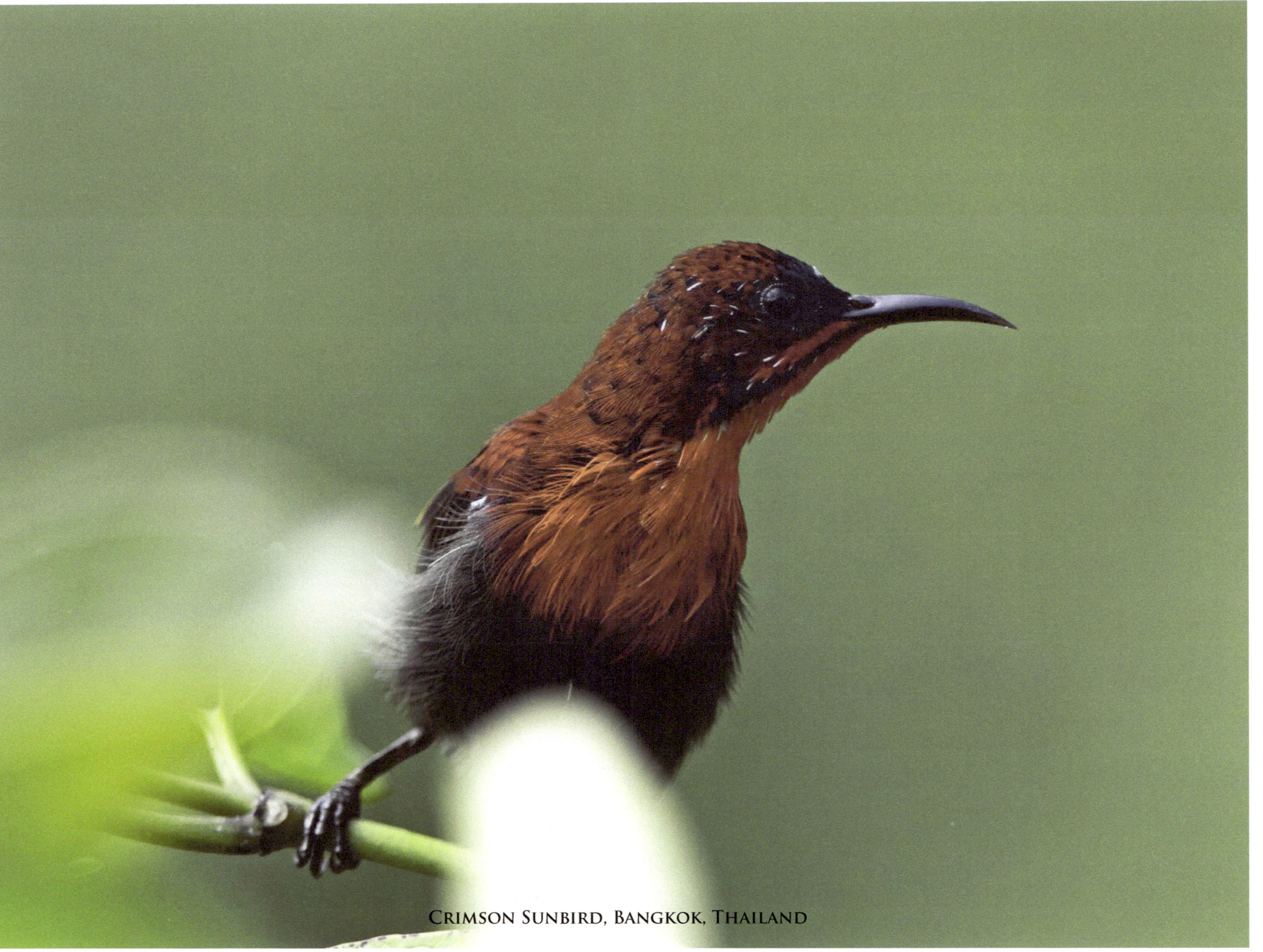

Crimson Sunbird, Bangkok, Thailand

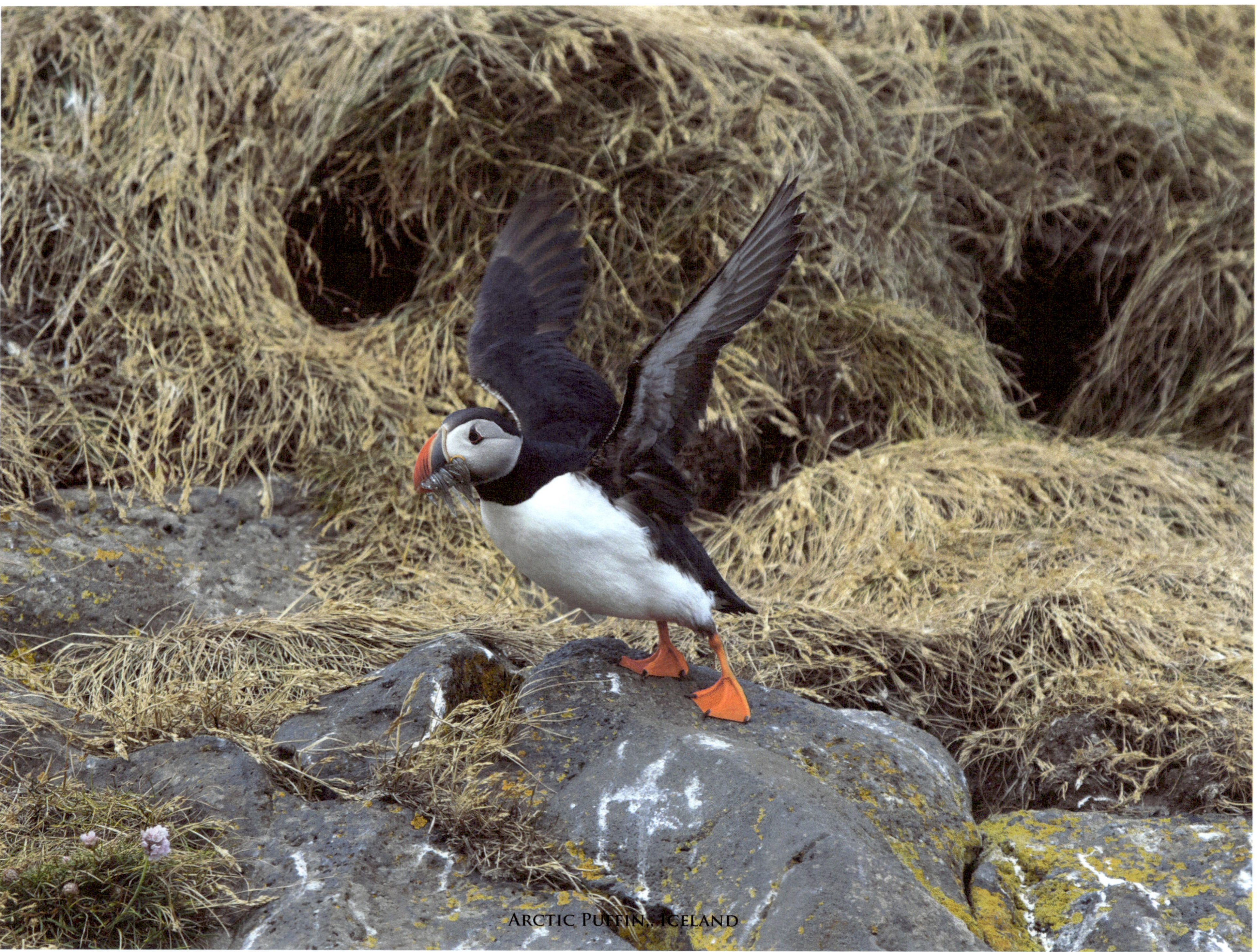

Arctic Puffin, Iceland

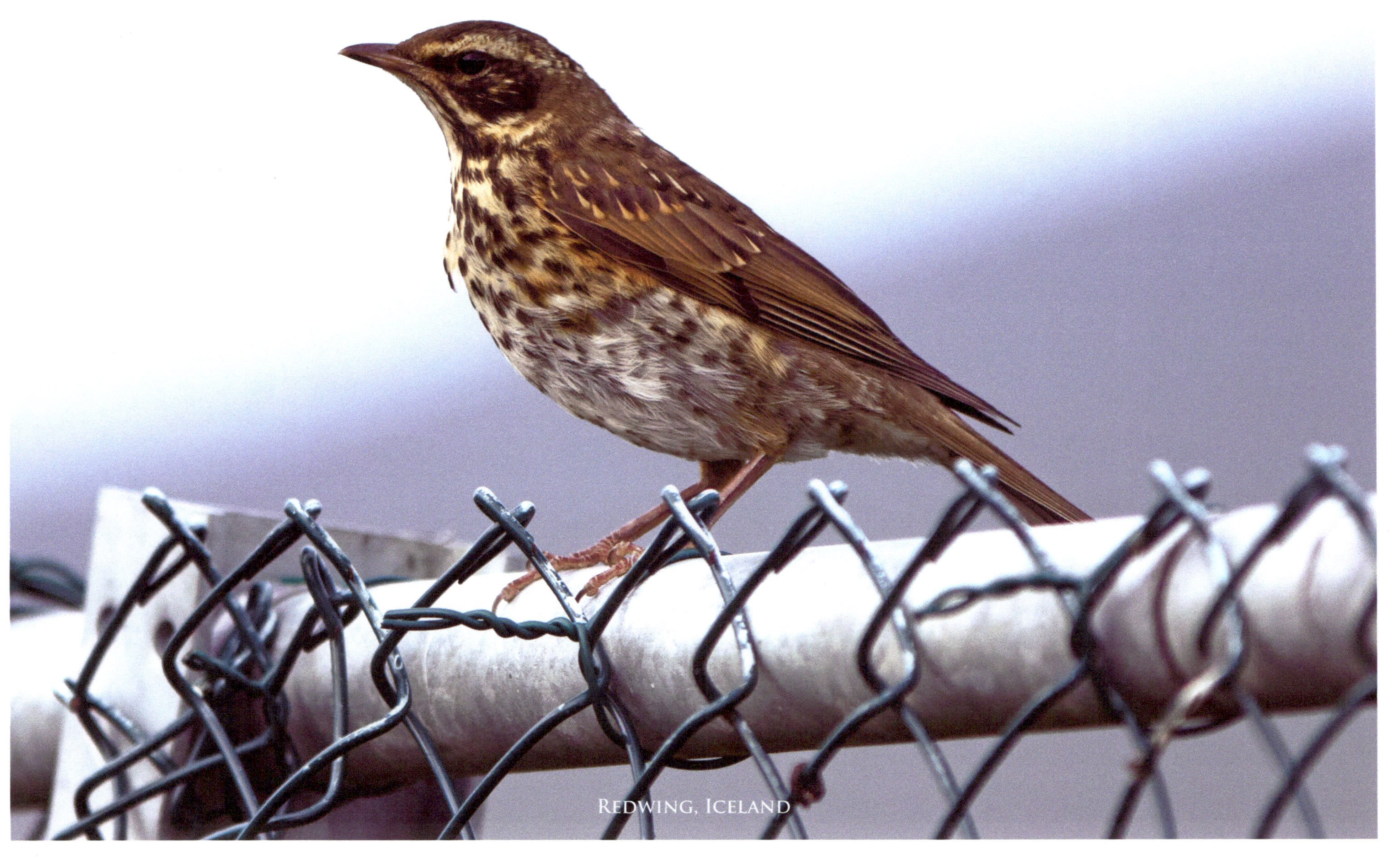

Redwing, Iceland

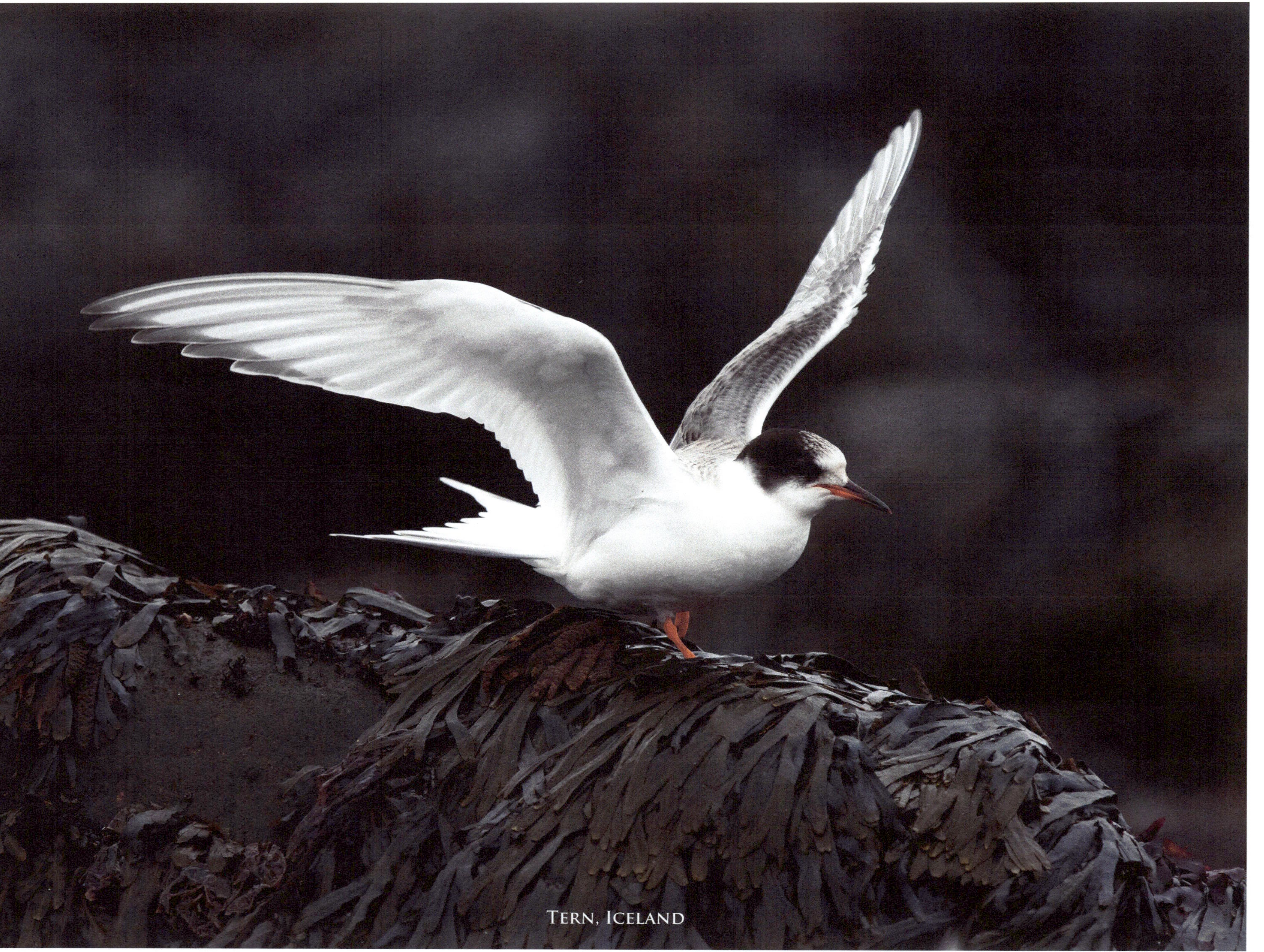

Tern, Iceland

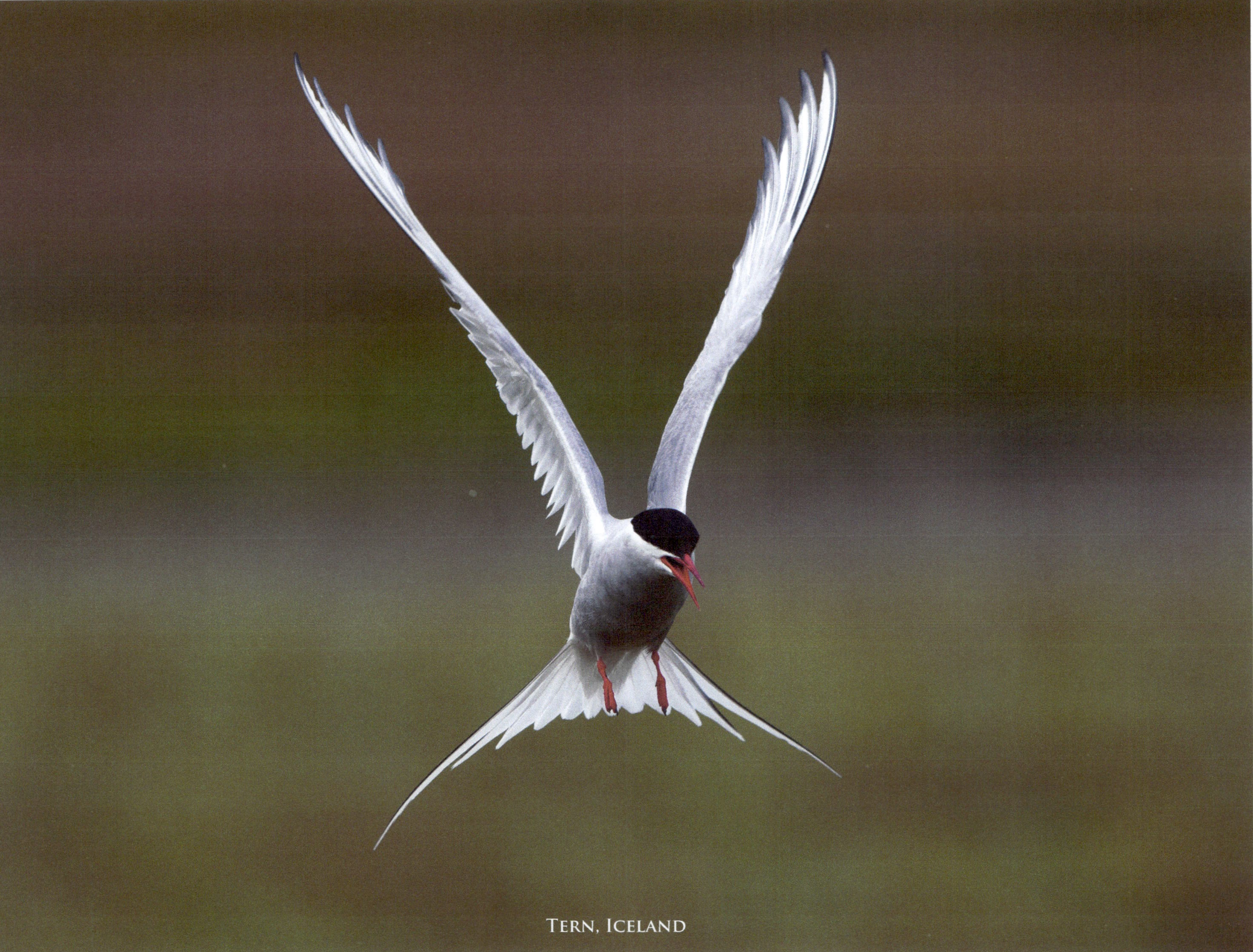

Tern, Iceland

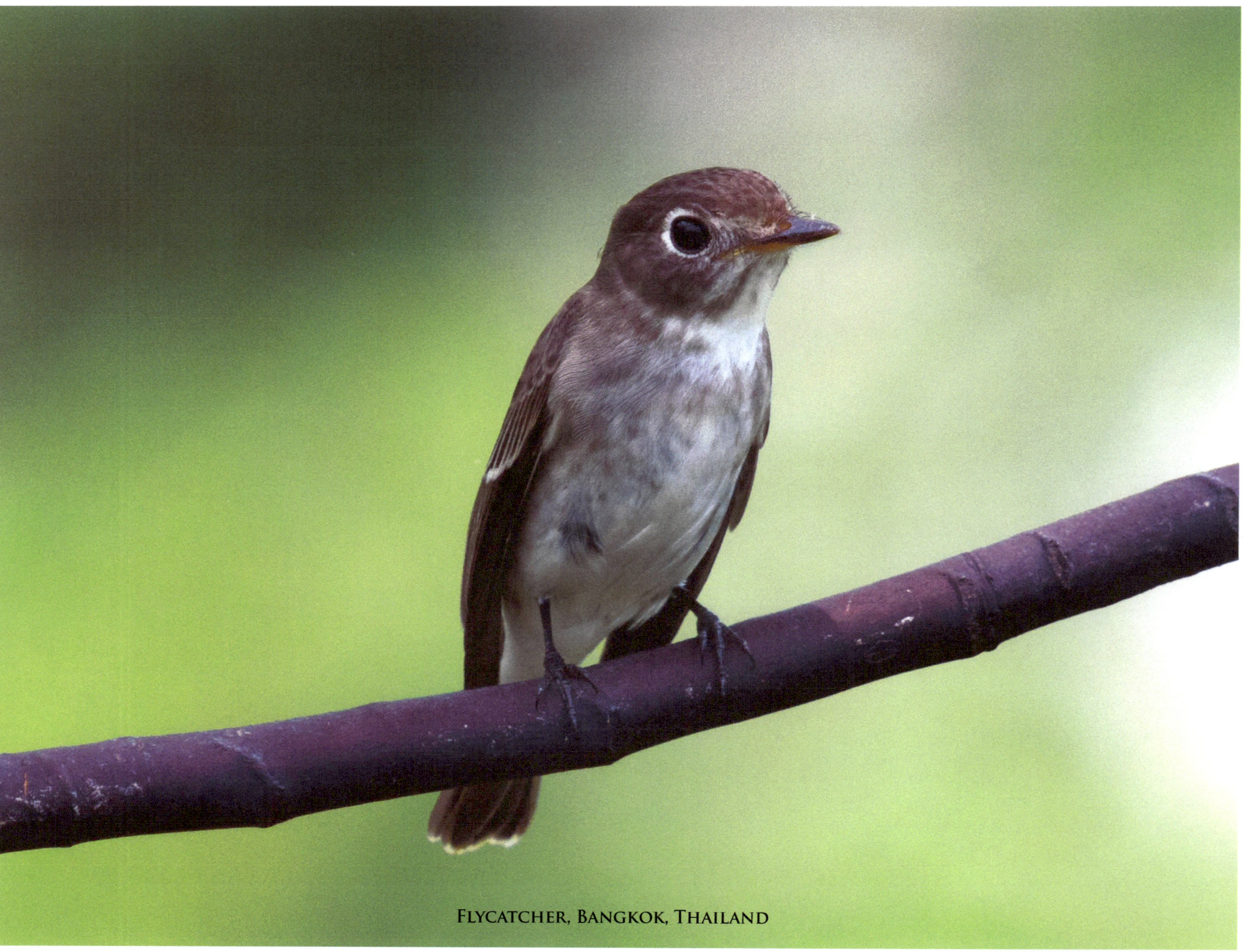

Flycatcher, Bangkok, Thailand

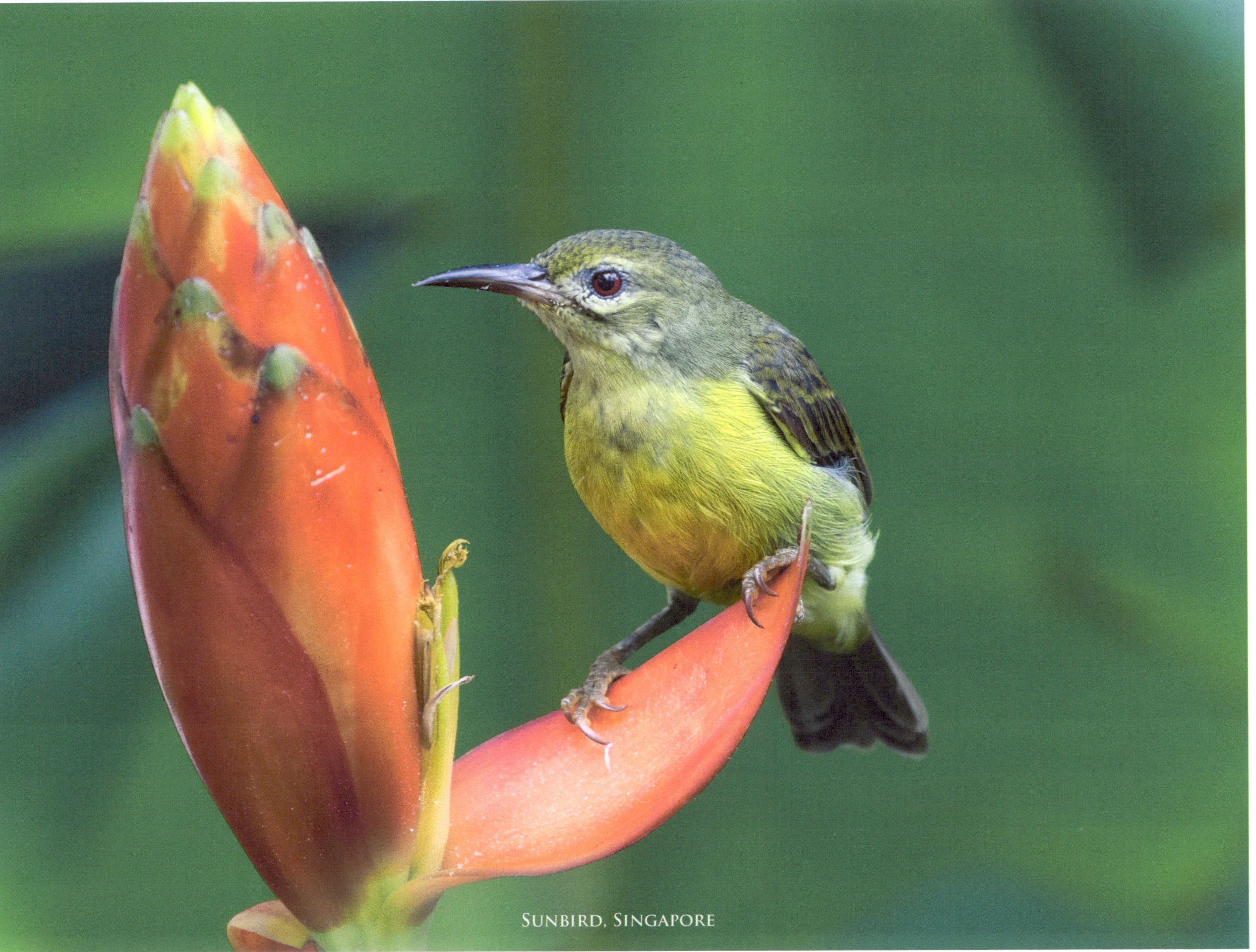

Sunbird, Singapore

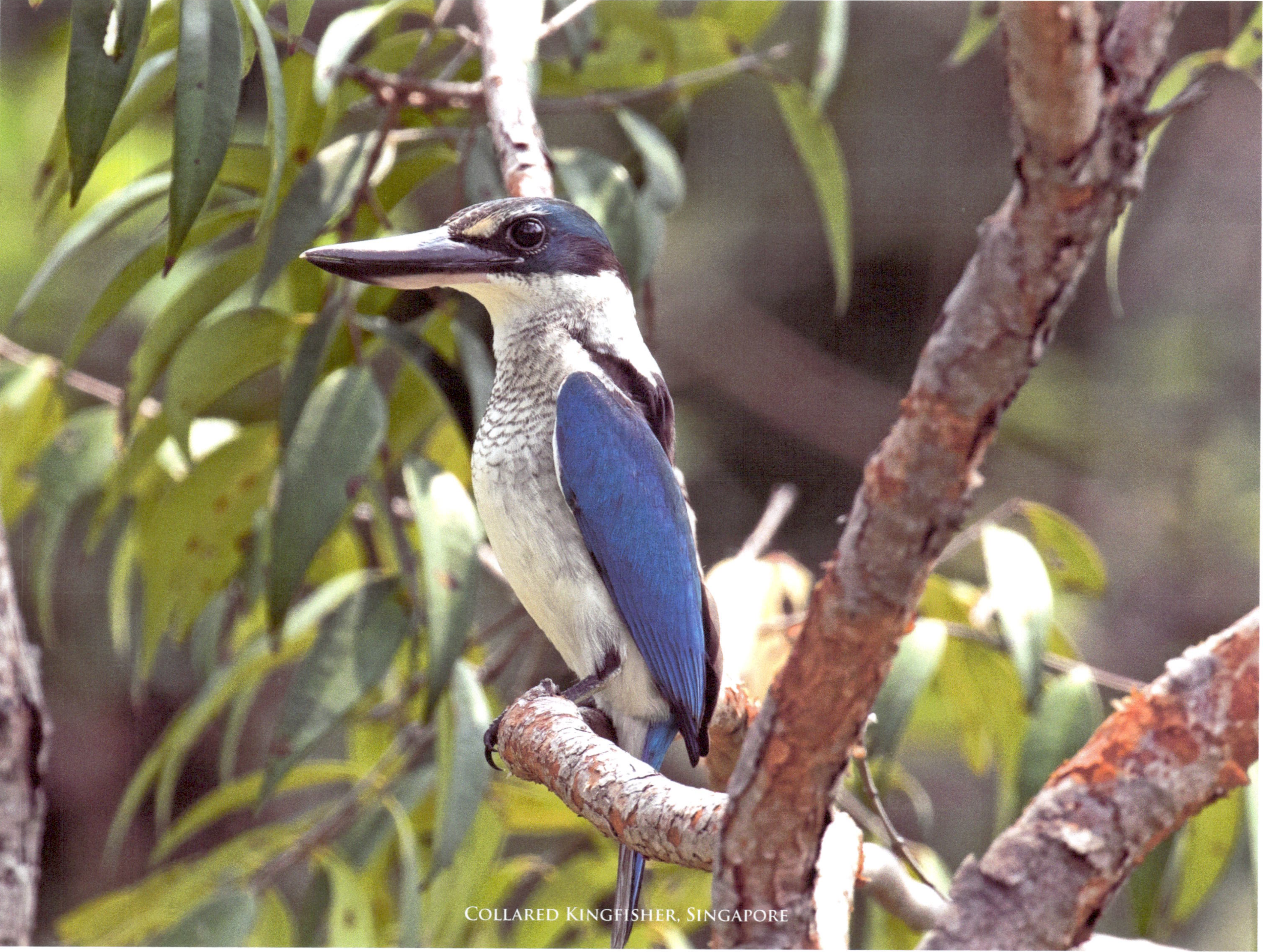

Collared Kingfisher, Singapore

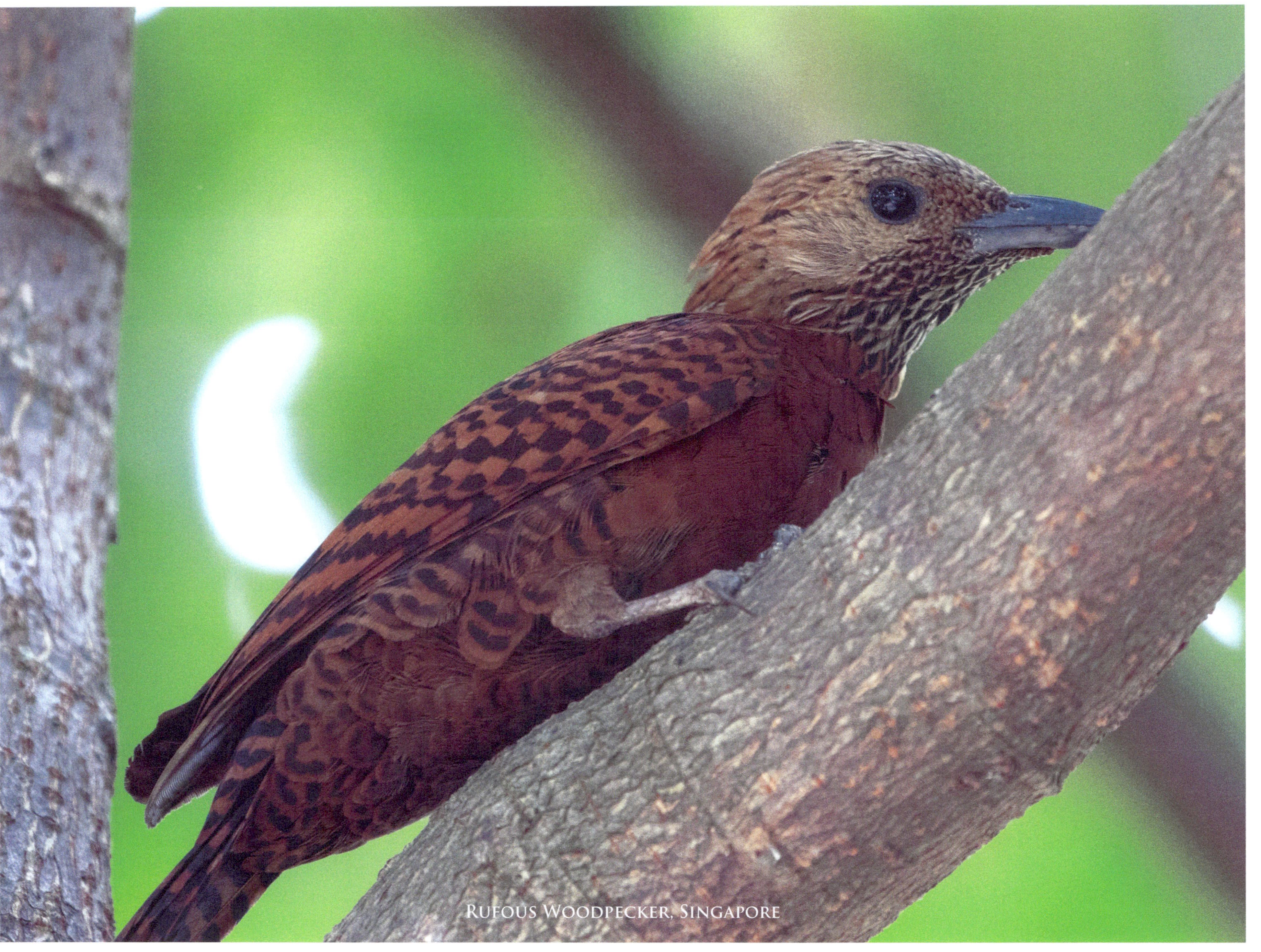

Rufous Woodpecker, Singapore

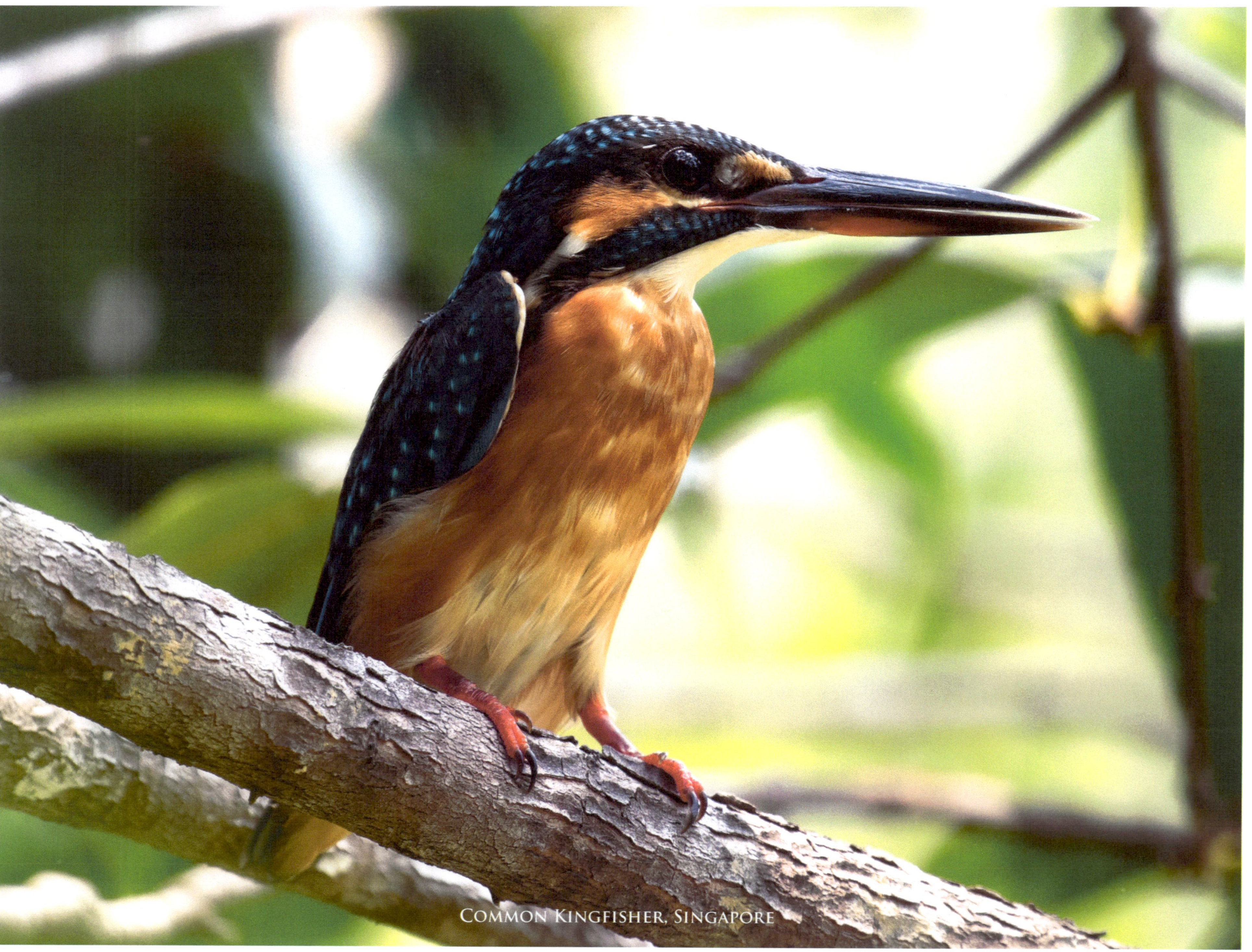

Common Kingfisher, Singapore

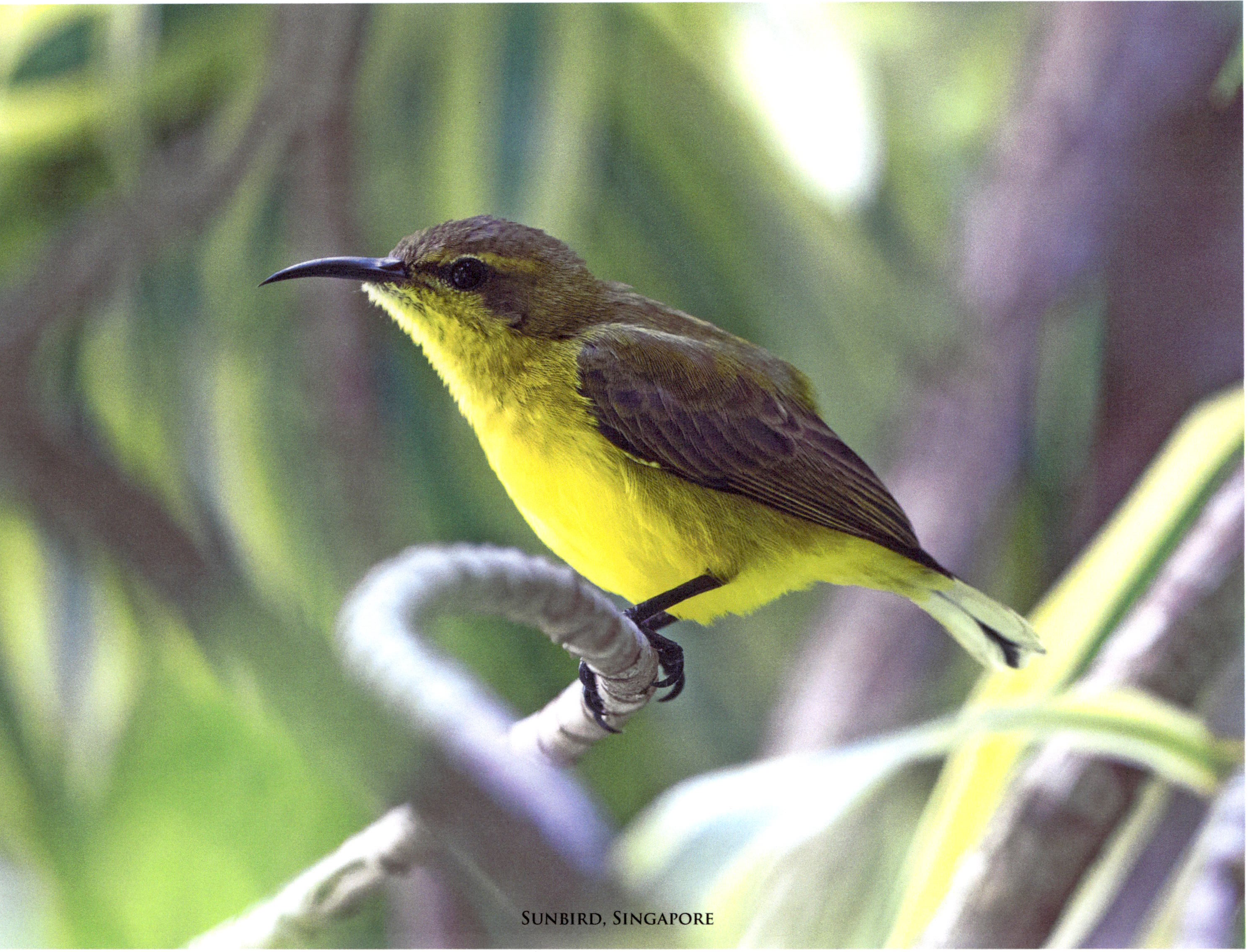

Sunbird, Singapore

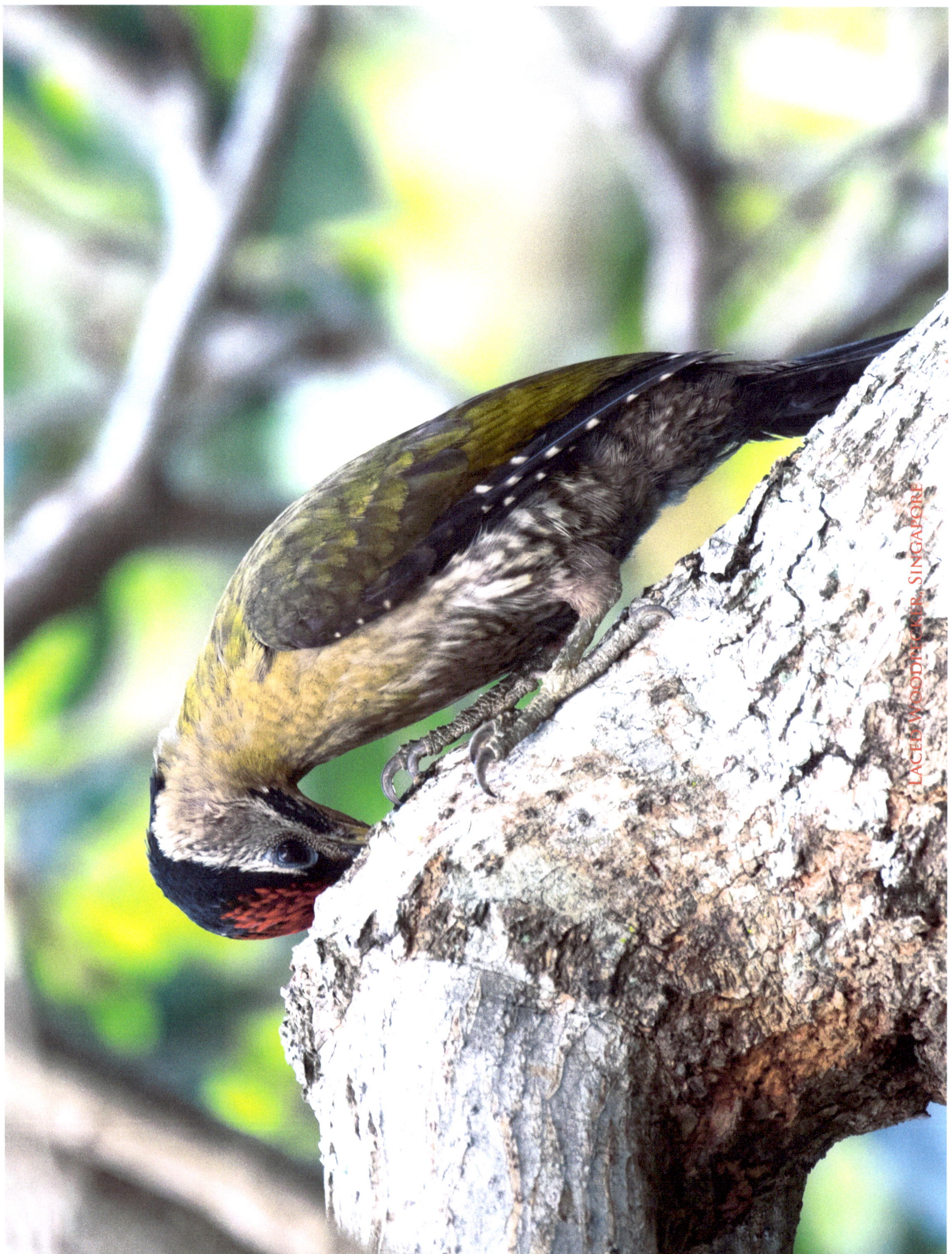

Laced Woodpecker, Singapore

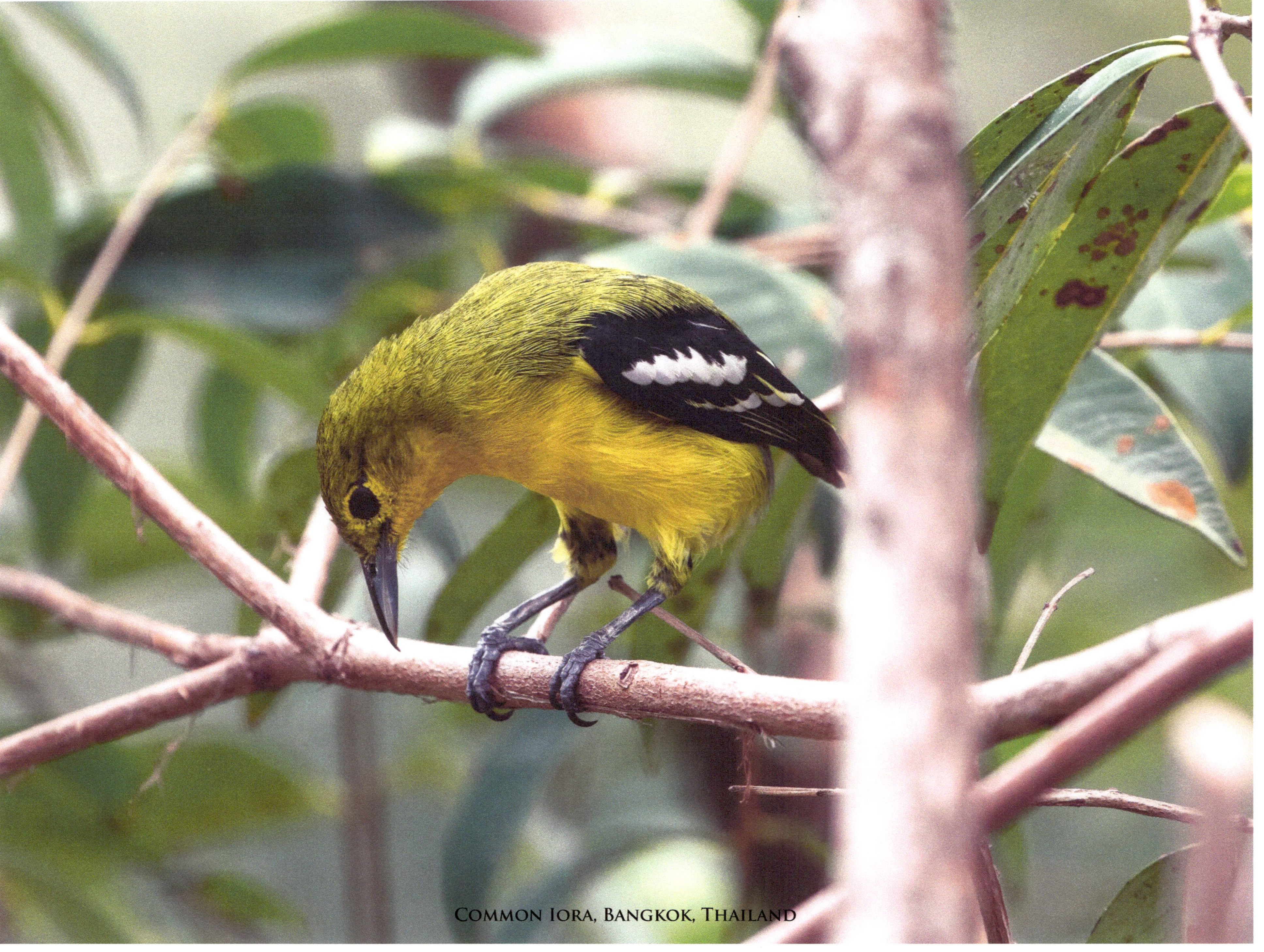

Common Iora, Bangkok, Thailand

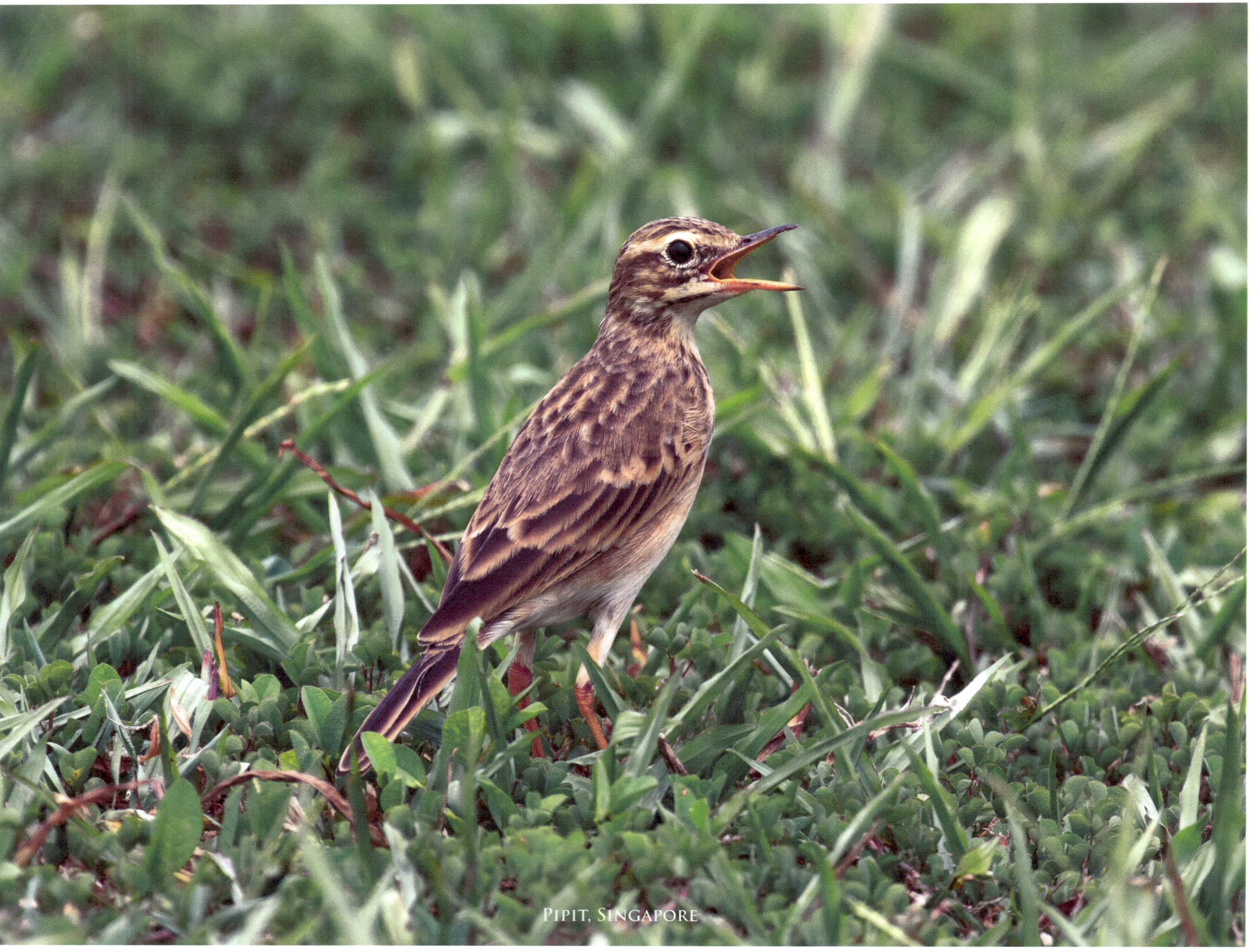

Pipit, Singapore

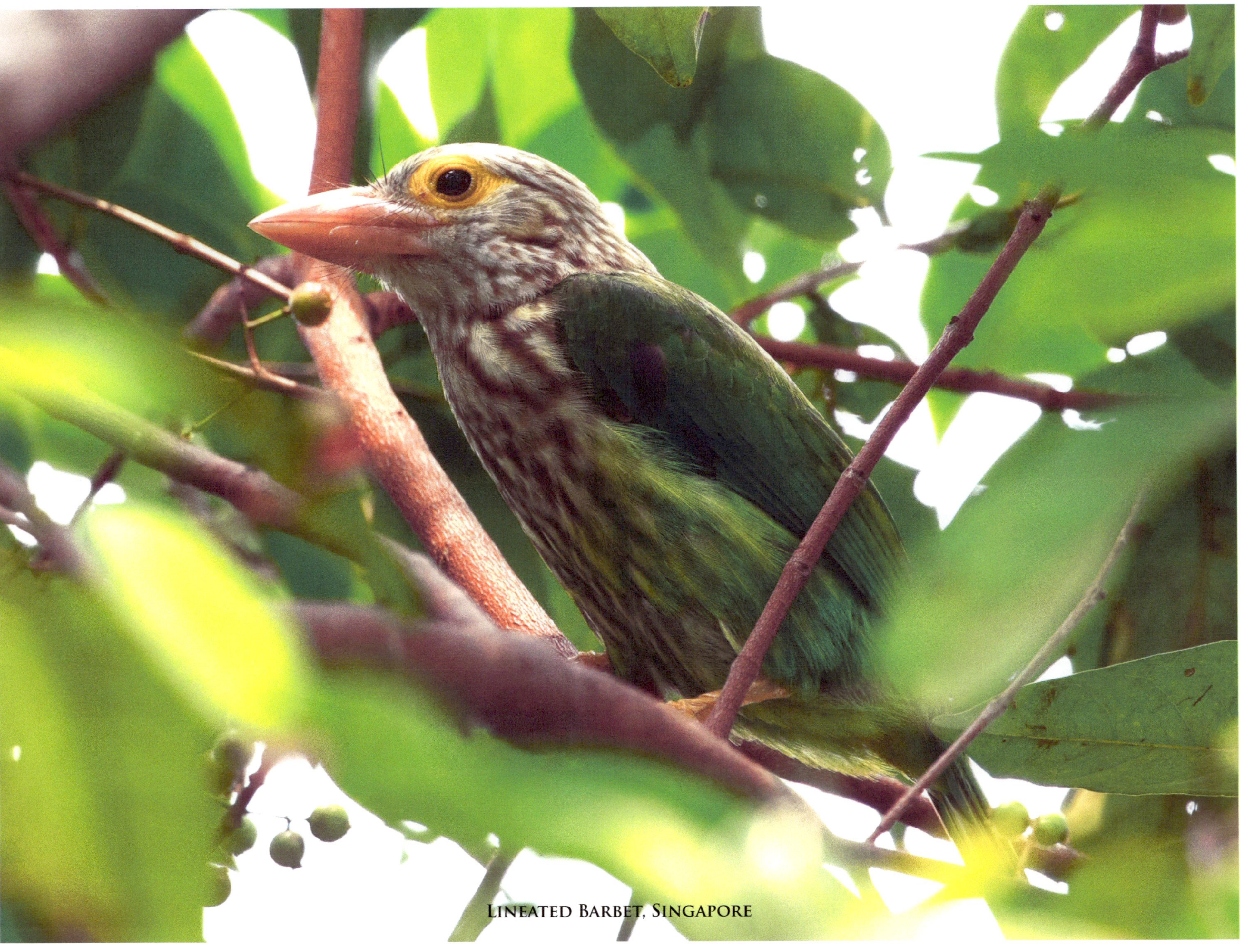

Lineated Barbet, Singapore

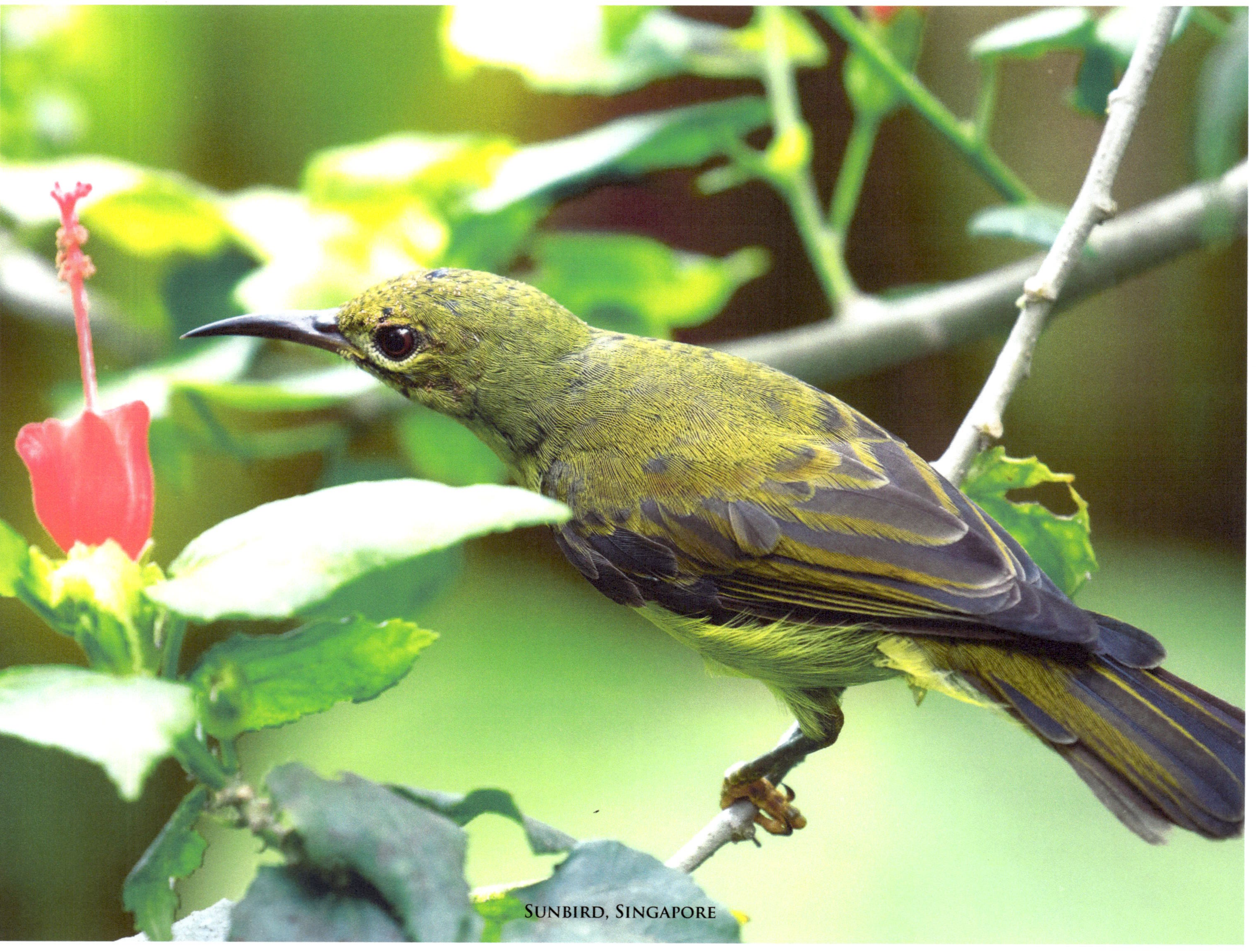

Sunbird, Singapore

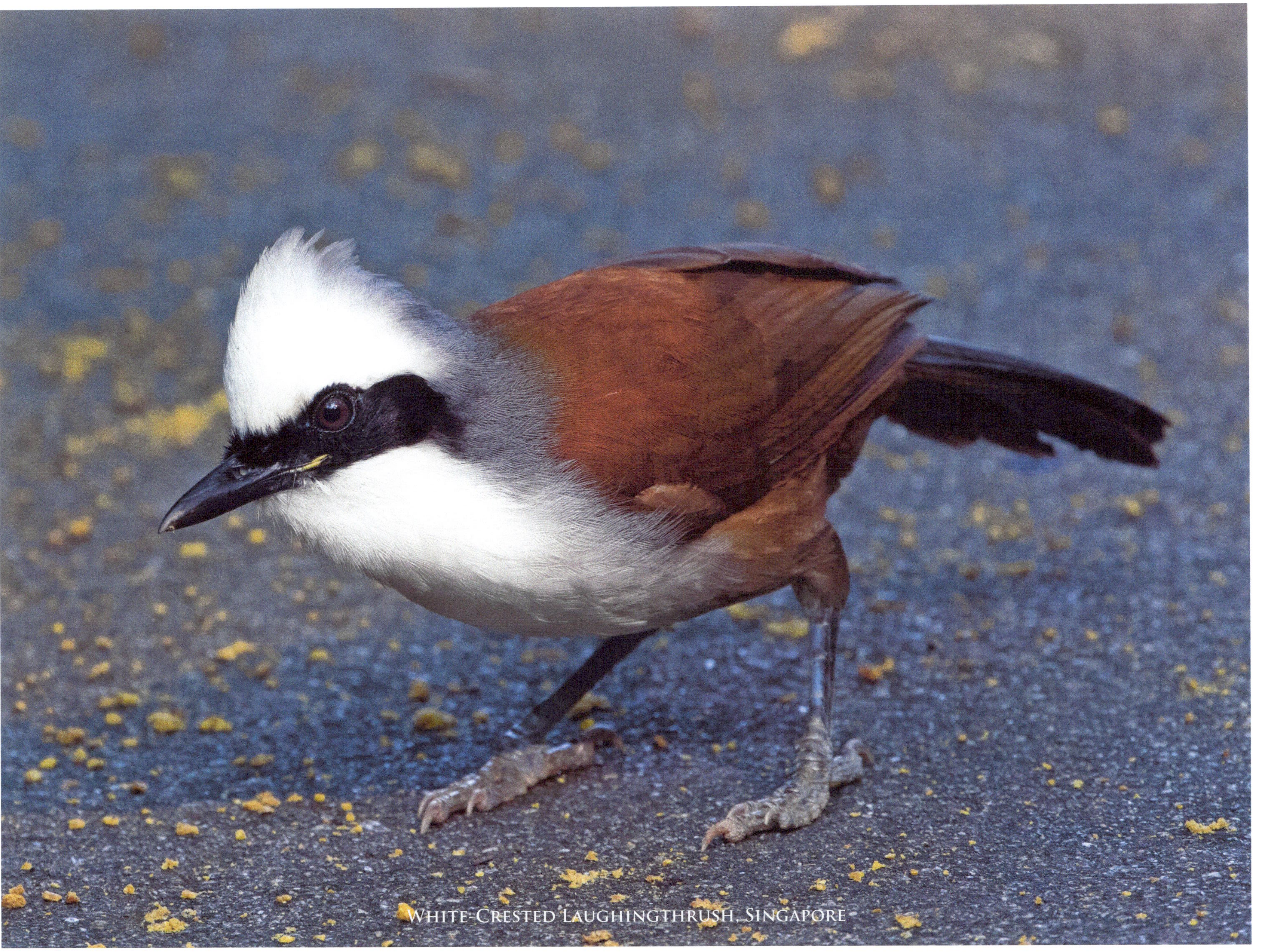

White-Crested Laughingthrush, Singapore

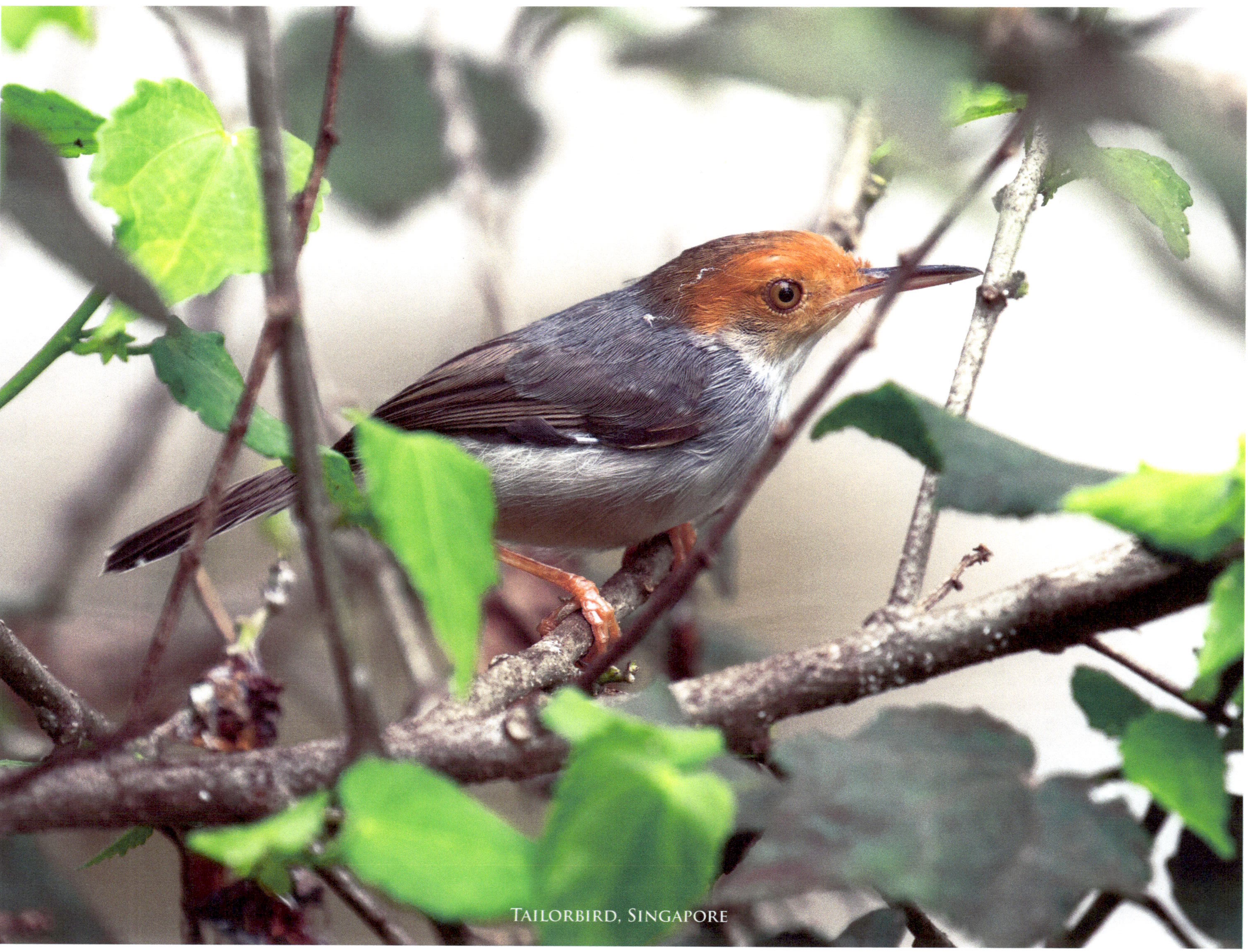

Tailorbird, Singapore

Common Kingfisher, Singapore

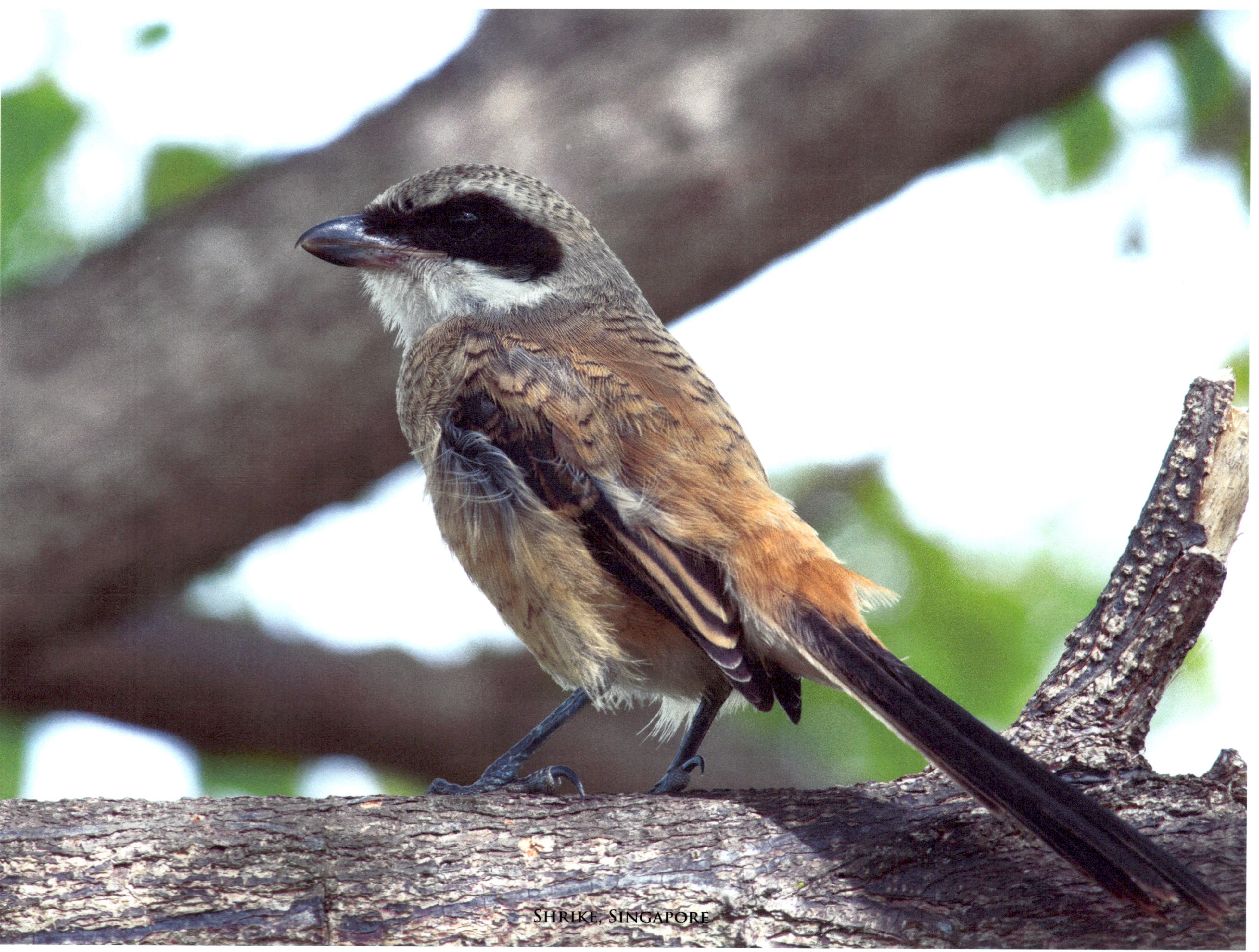

Shrike, Singapore

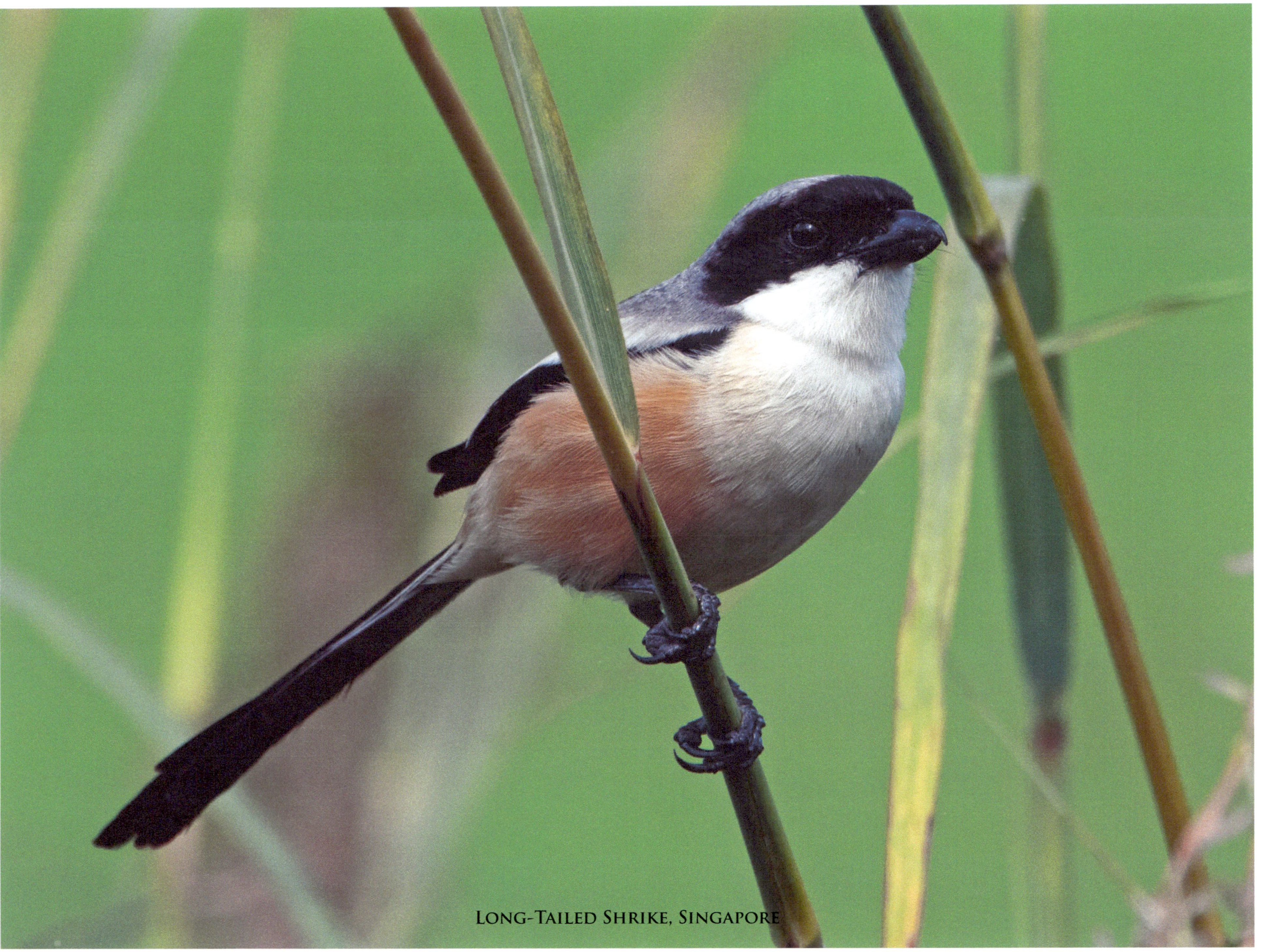

Long-Tailed Shrike, Singapore

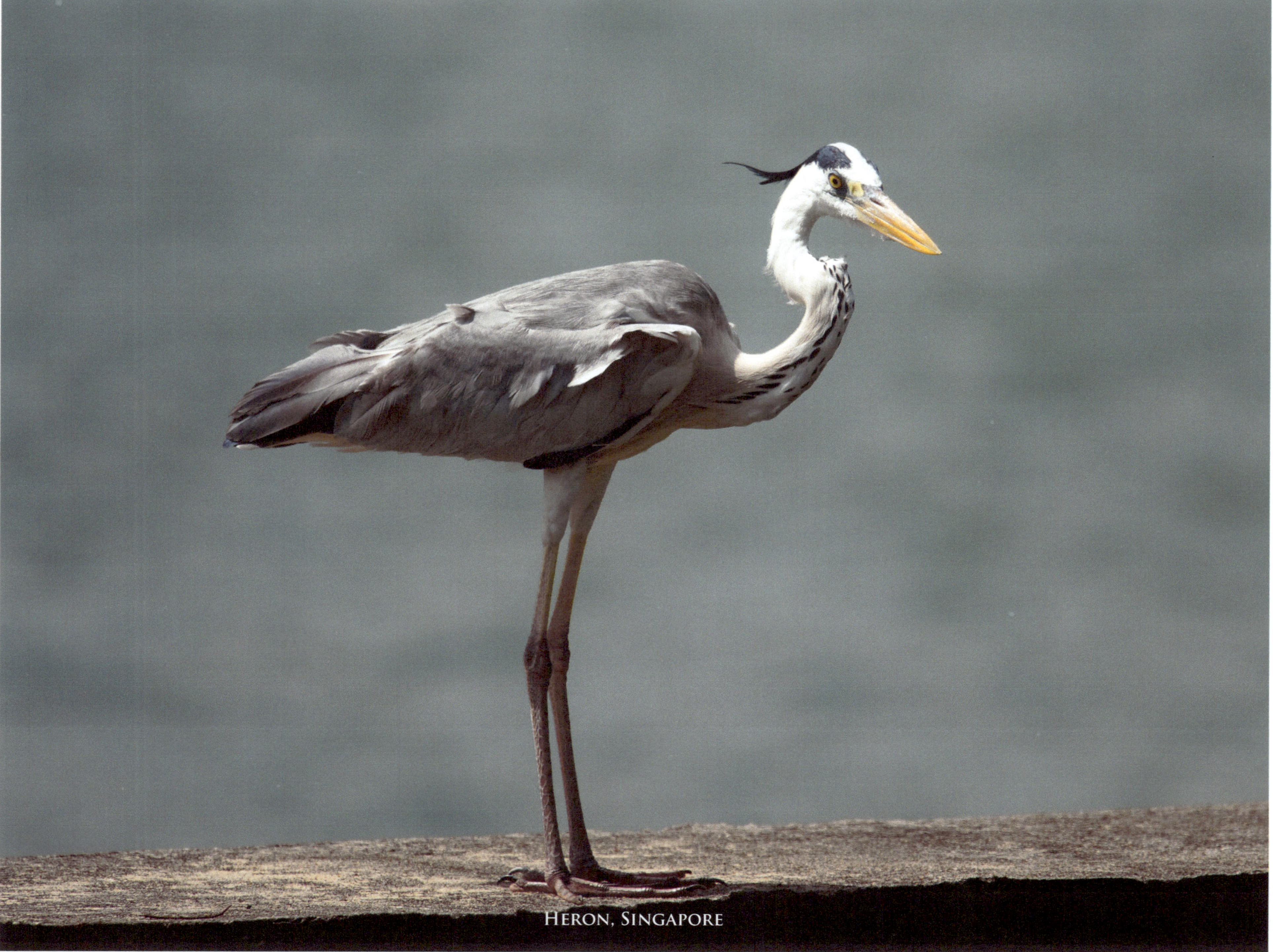

Heron, Singapore

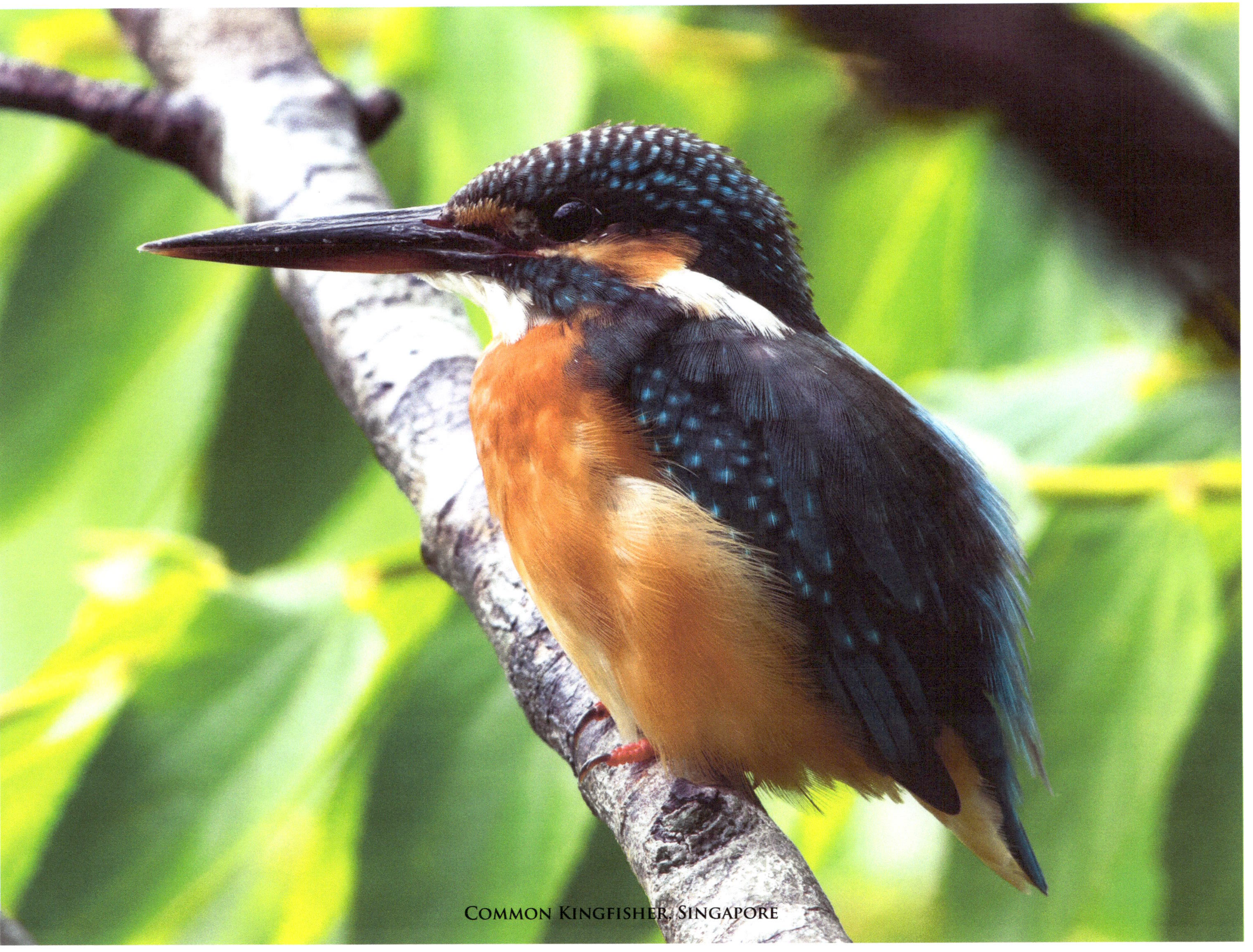

Common Kingfisher, Singapore

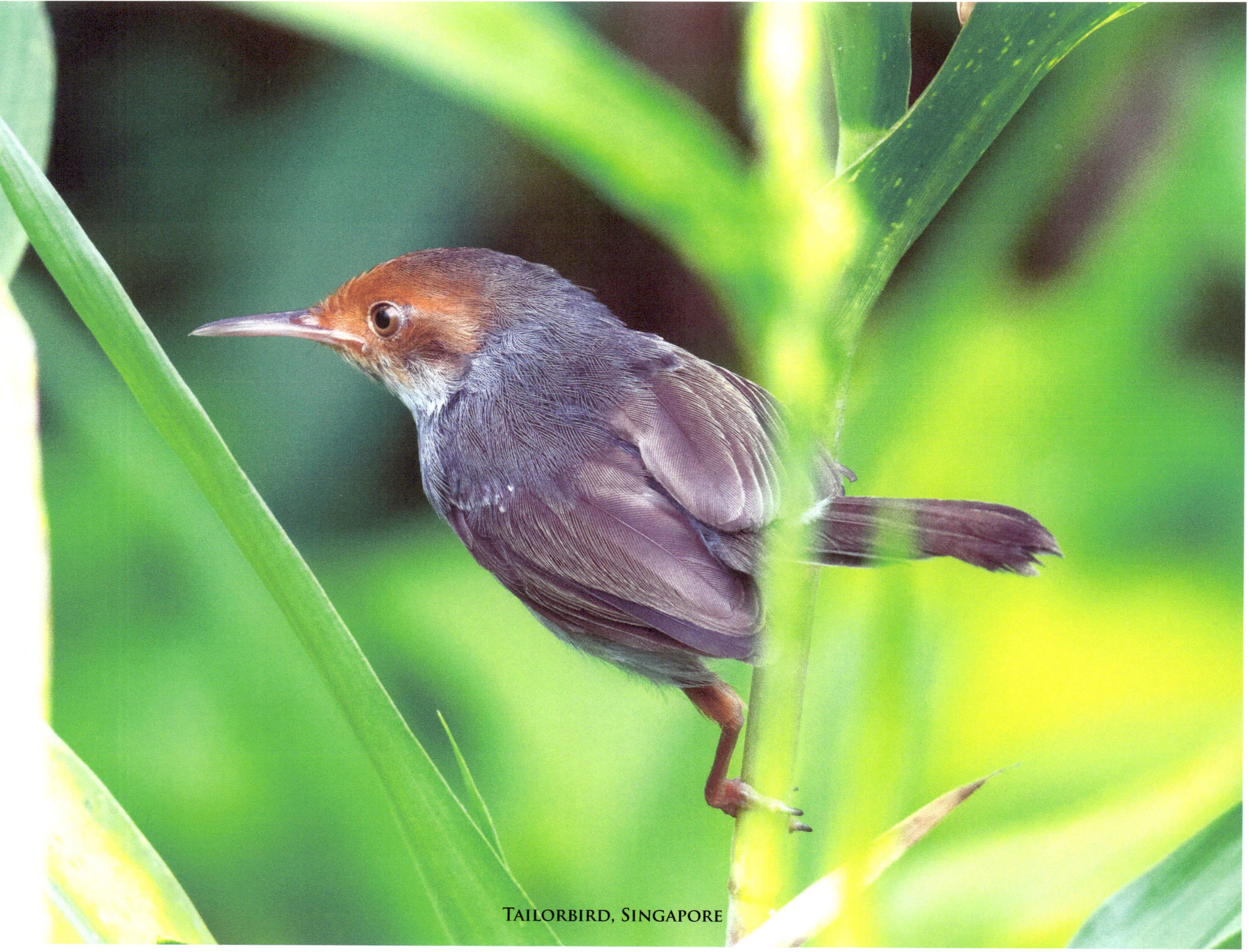

Tailorbird, Singapore

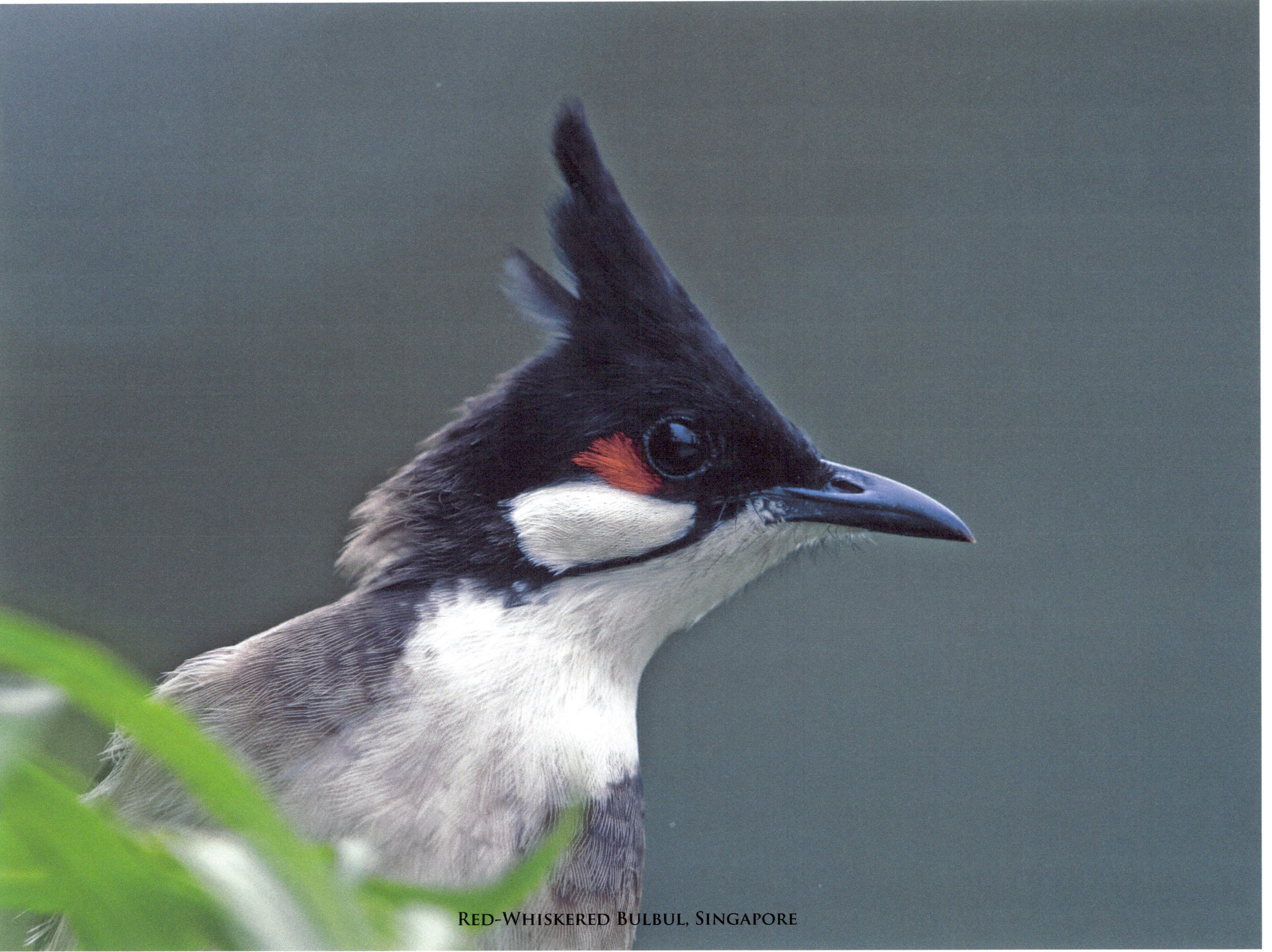

Red-Whiskered Bulbul, Singapore

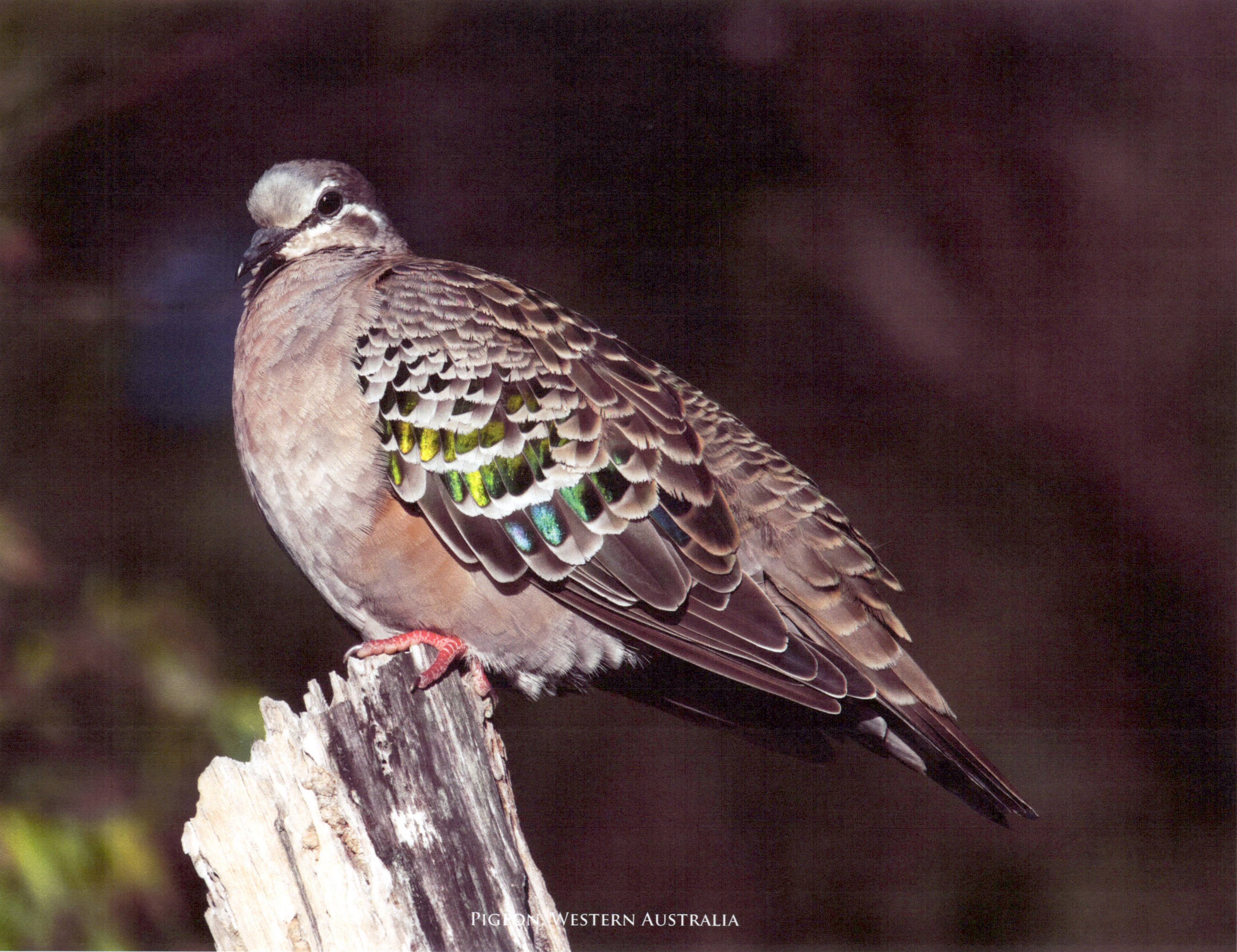

PIGEON, WESTERN AUSTRALIA

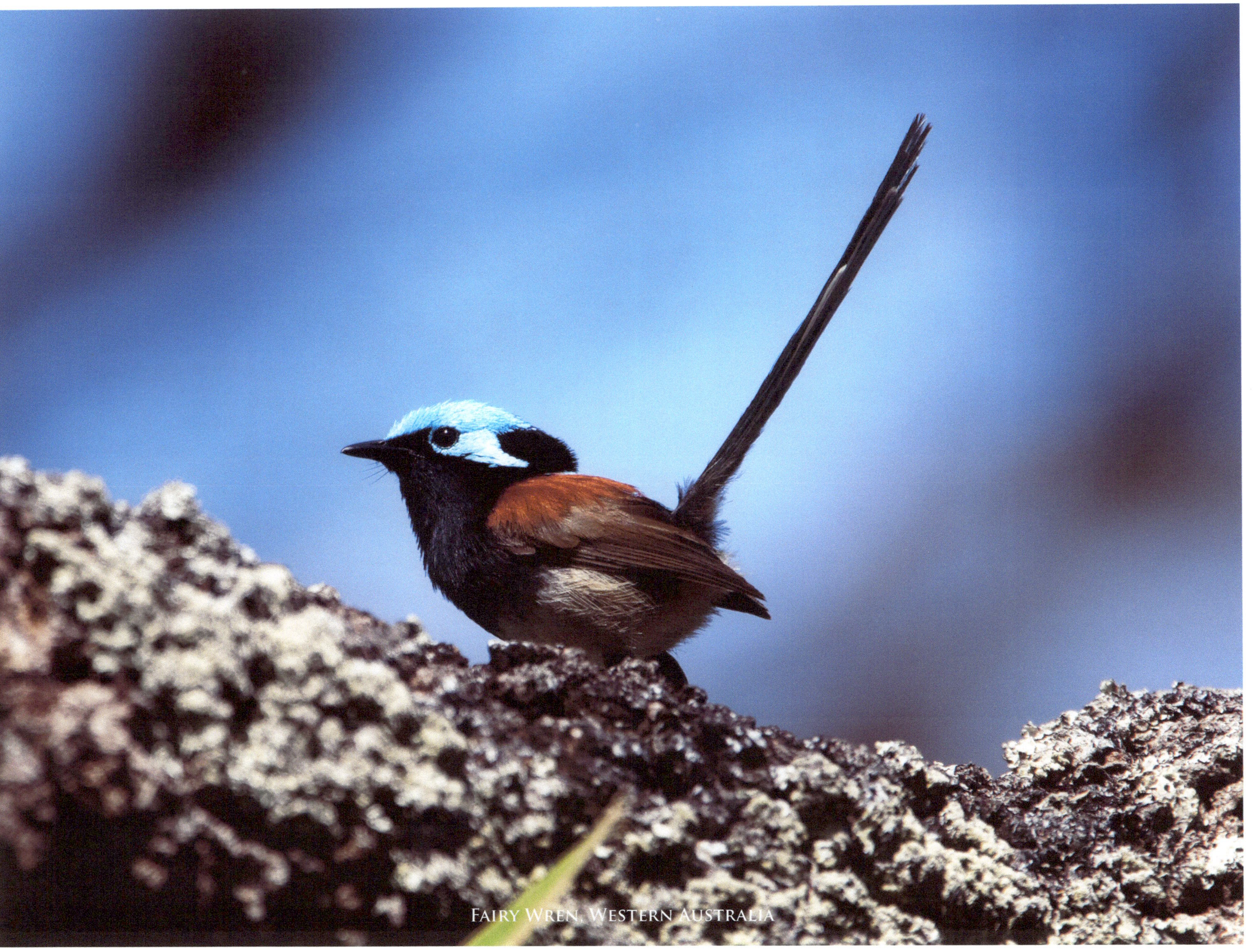

Fairy Wren, Western Australia

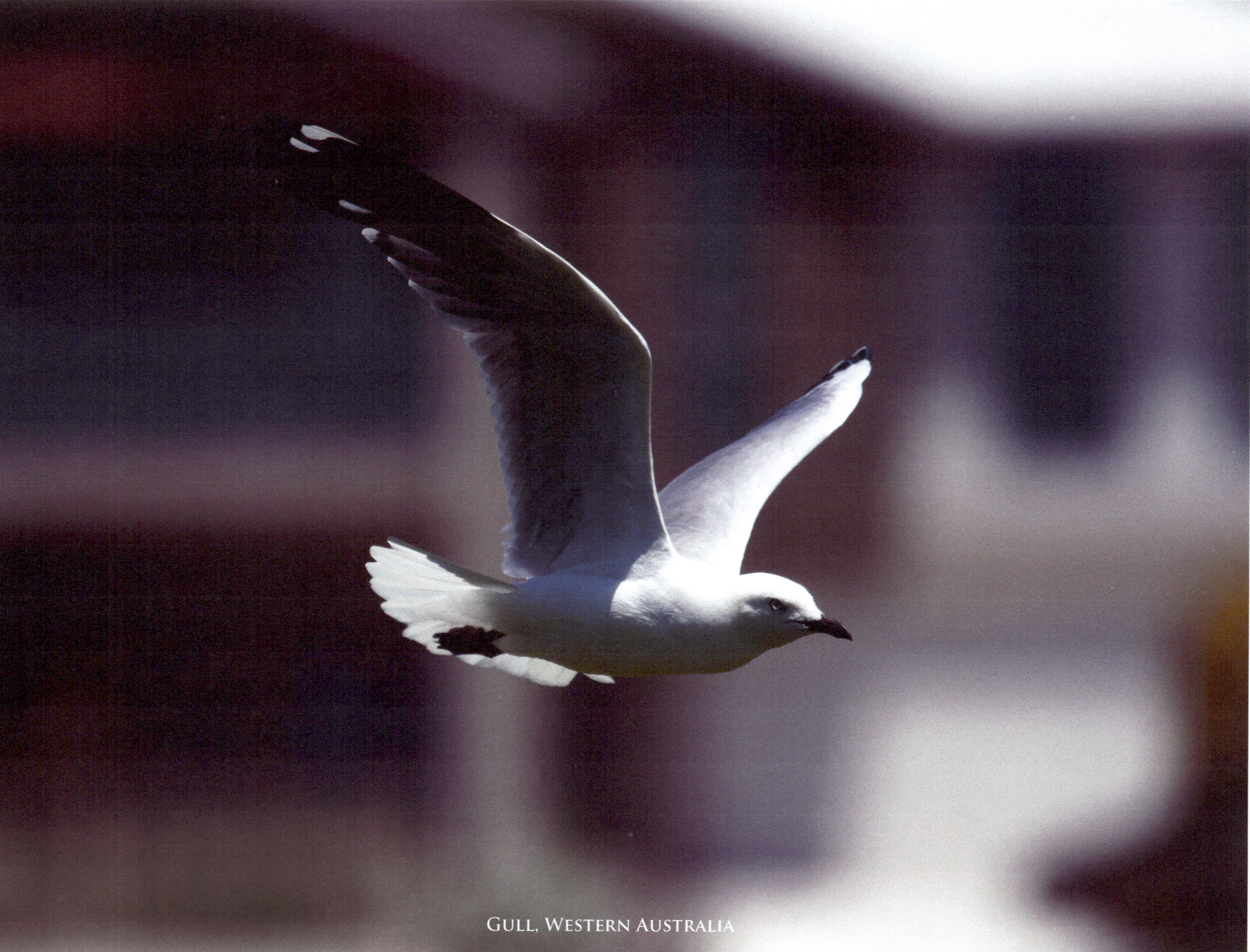

GULL, WESTERN AUSTRALIA

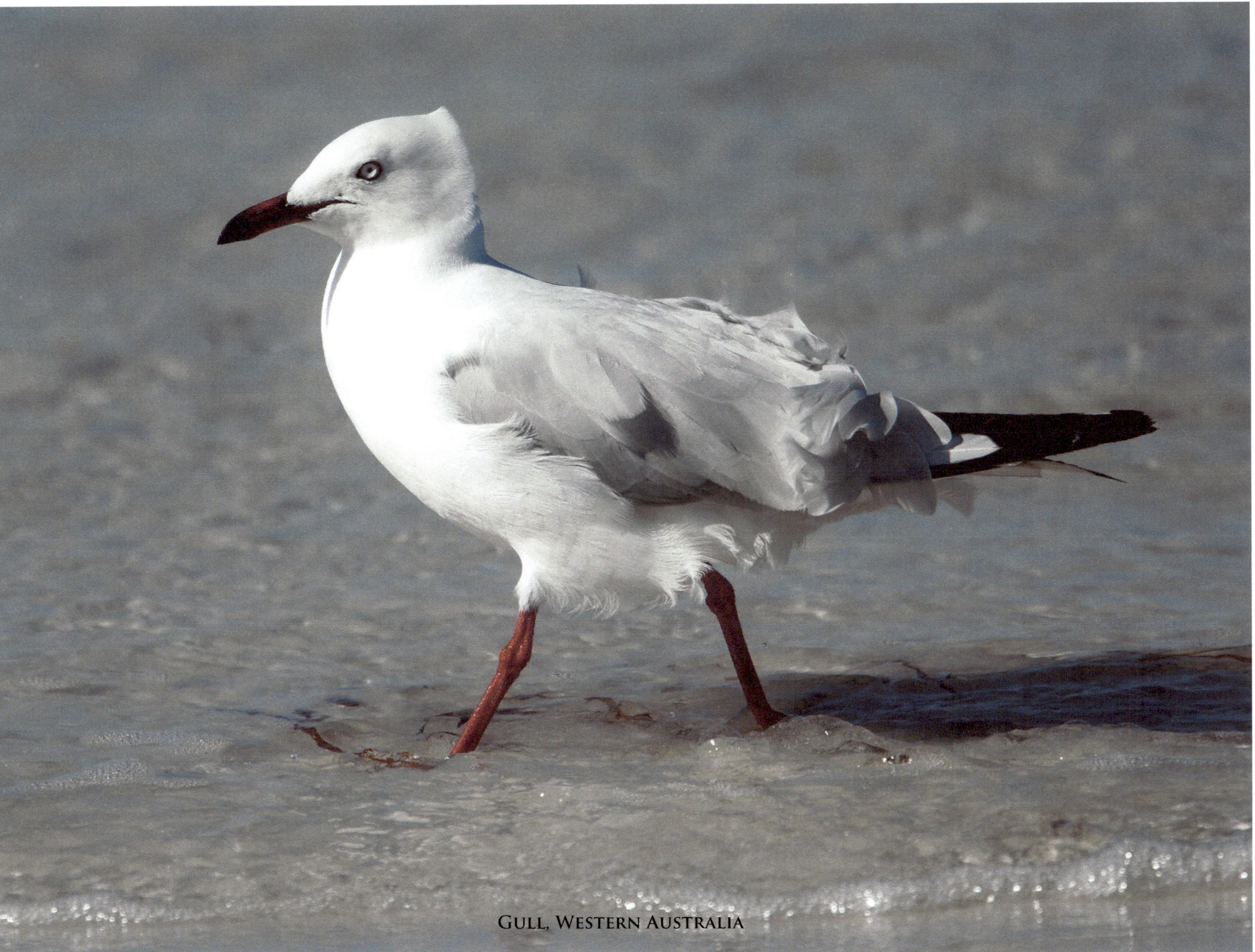

Gull, Western Australia

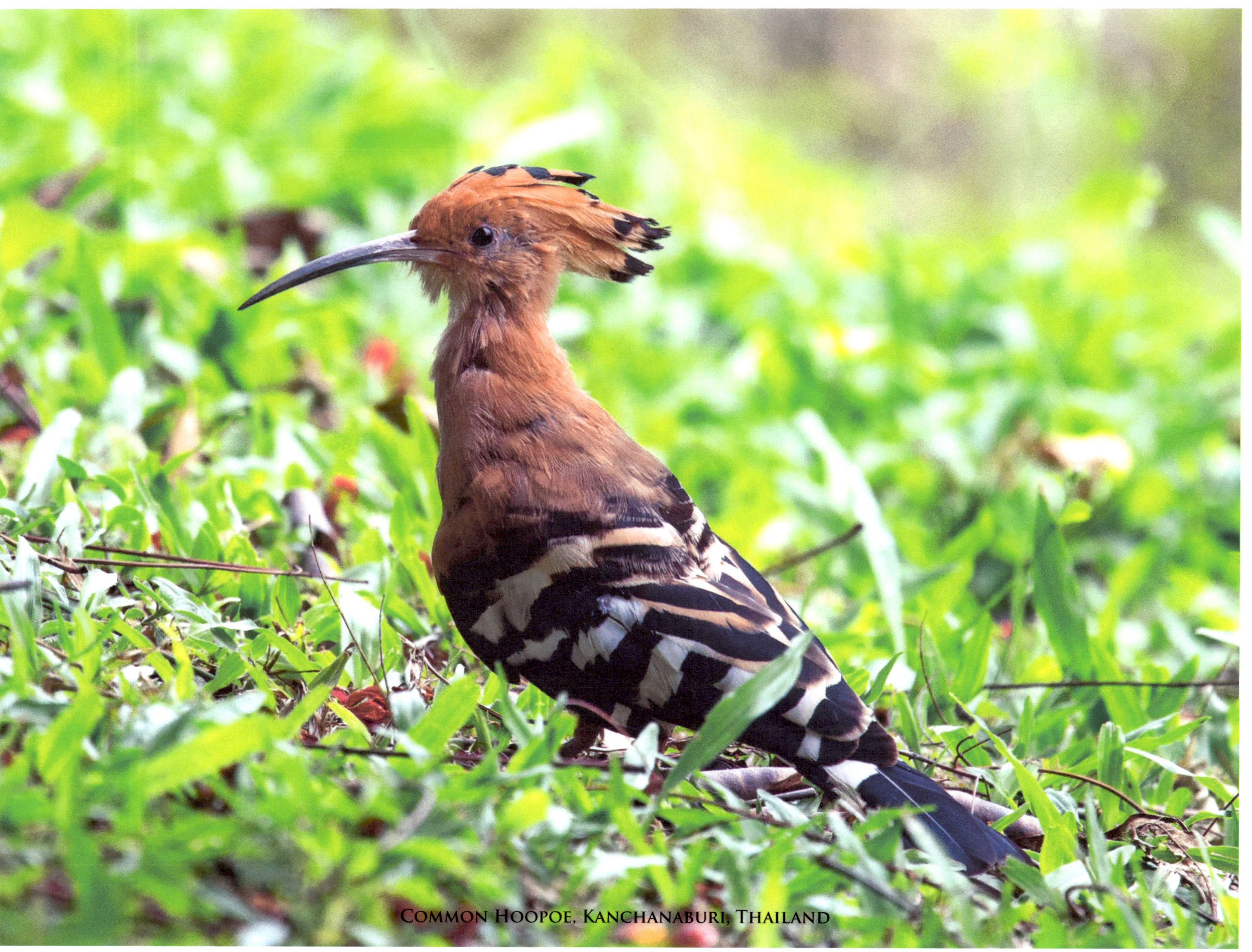

Common Hoopoe, Kanchanaburi, Thailand

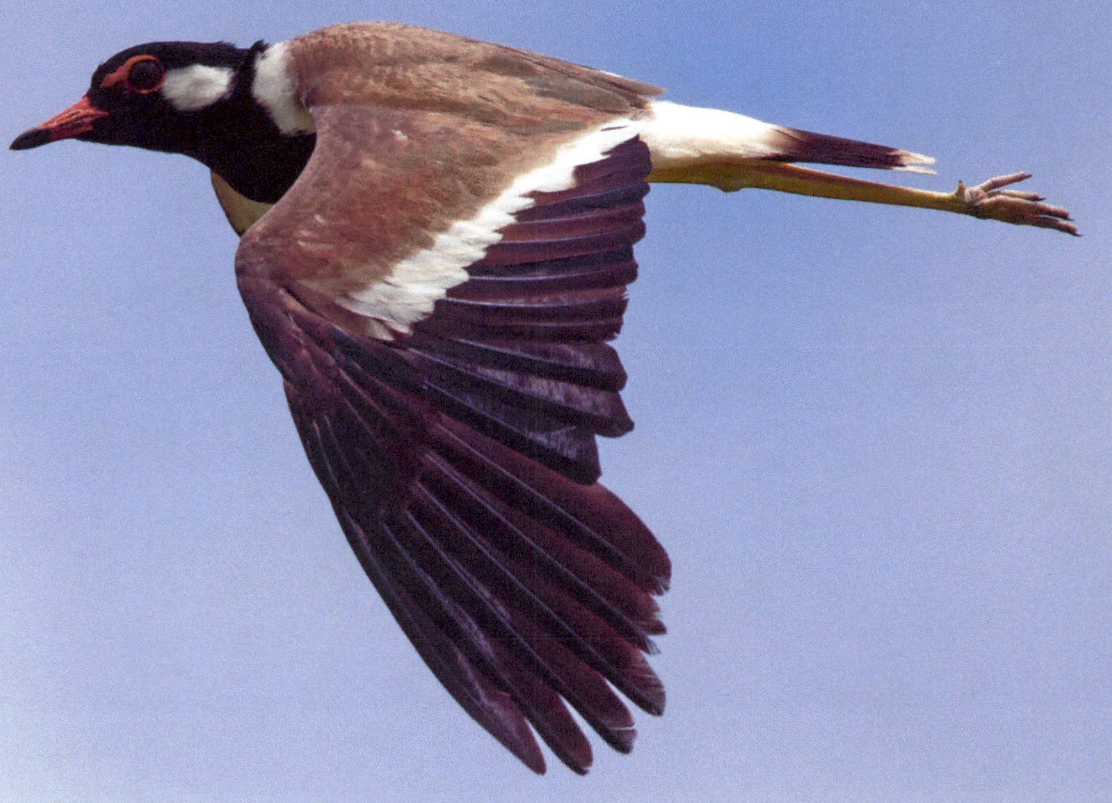

Red-Wattled Lapwing, Kanchanaburi, Thailand

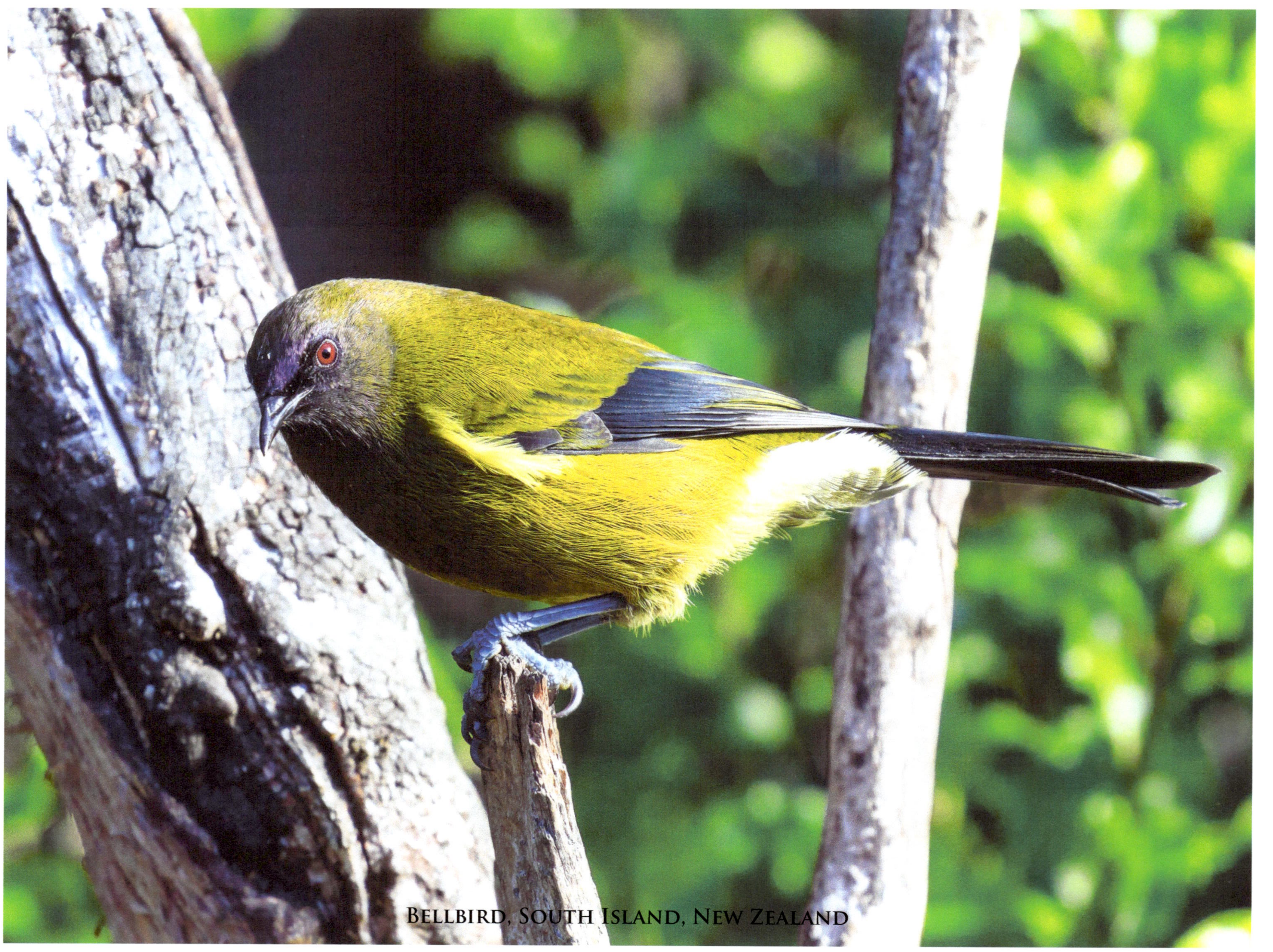

Bellbird, South Island, New Zealand

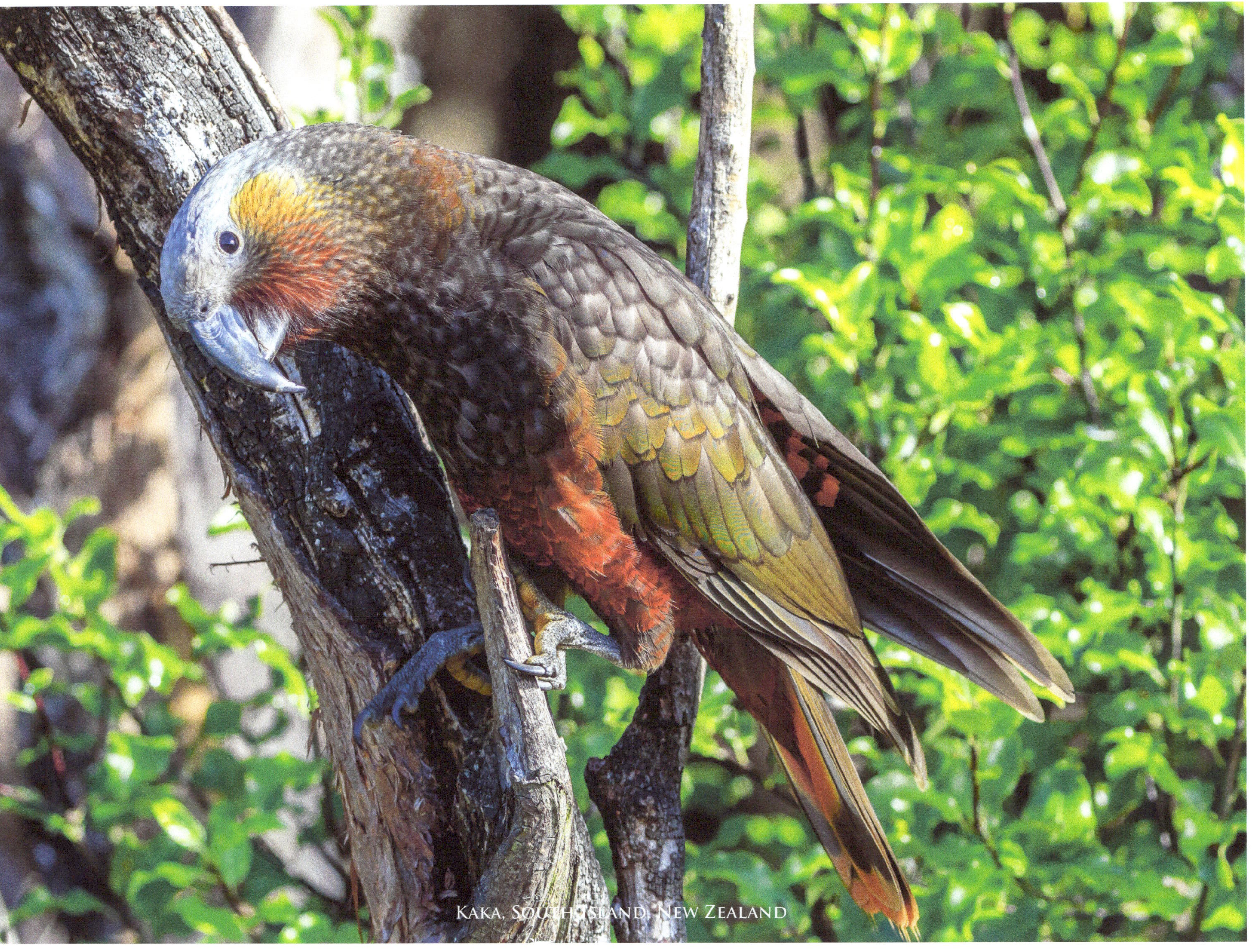

Kaka, South Island, New Zealand

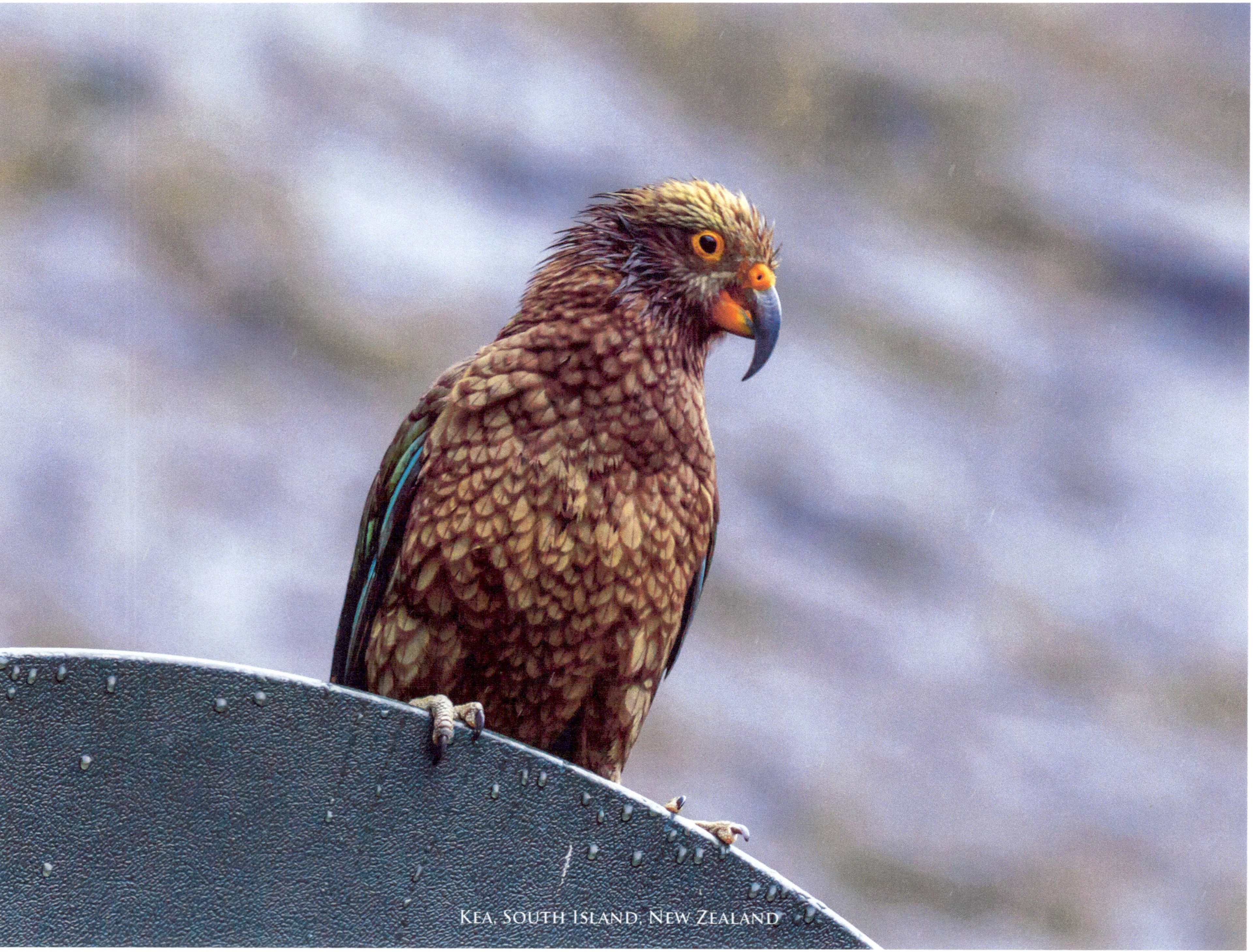

Kea, South Island, New Zealand

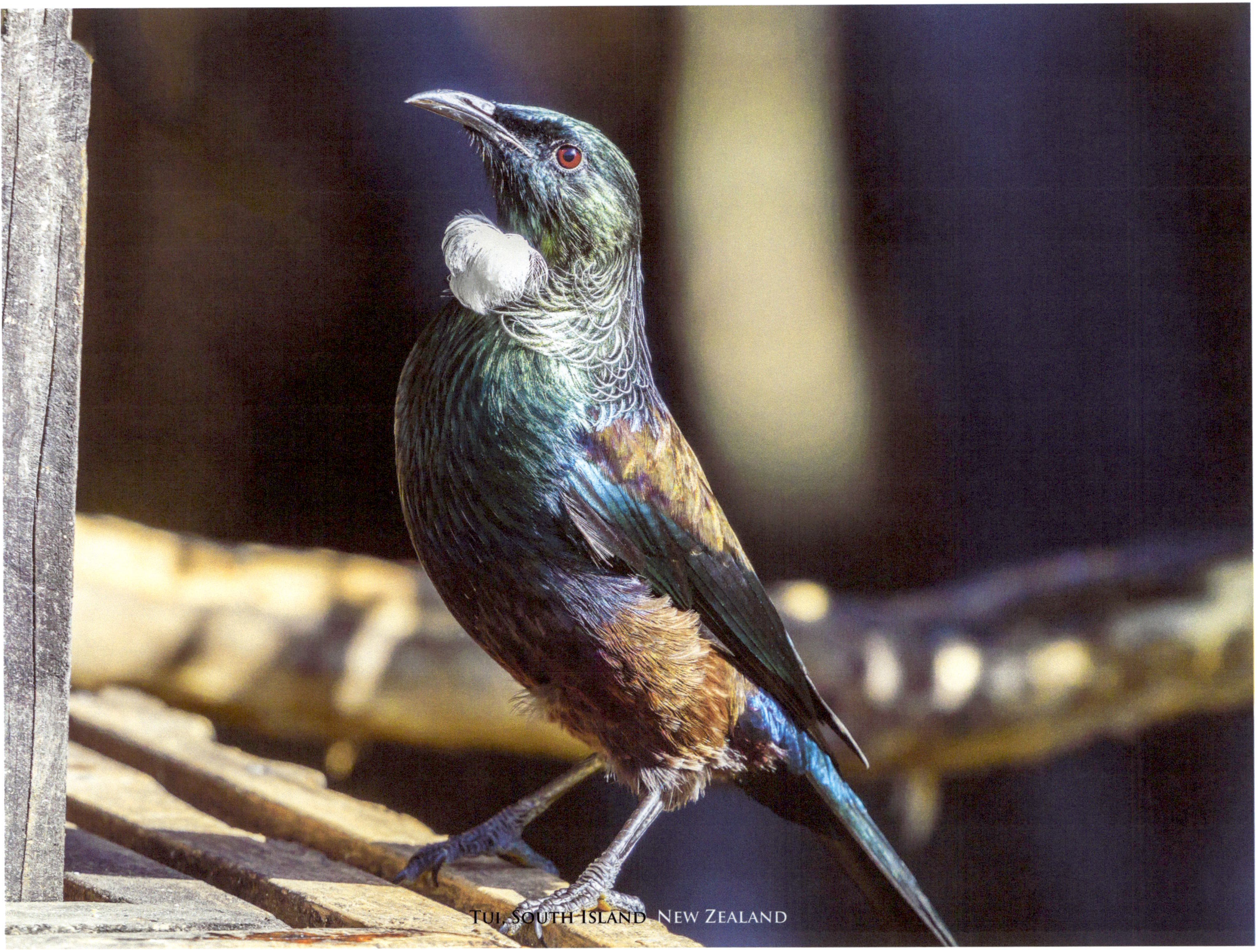

Tui, South Island New Zealand

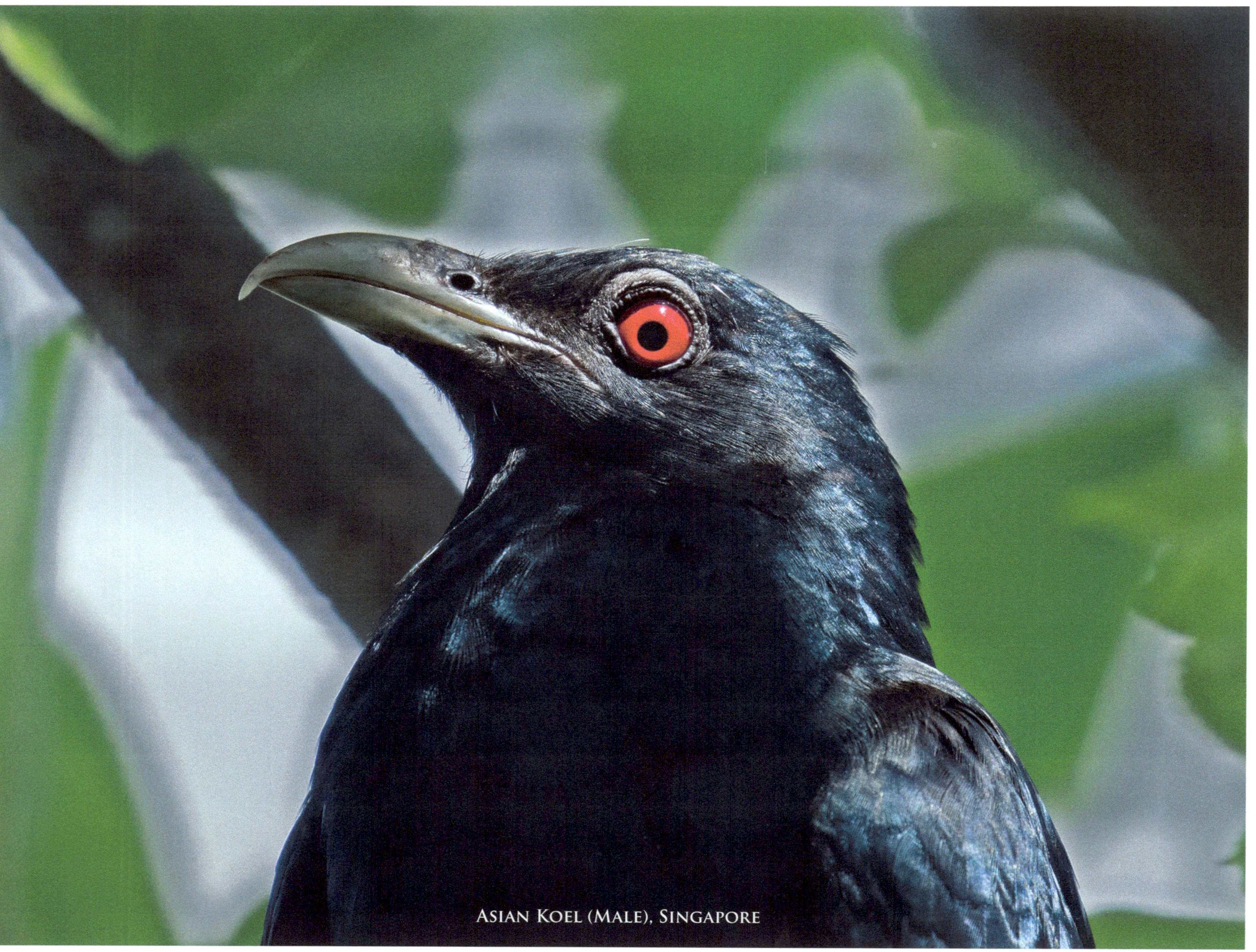

Asian Koel (Male), Singapore

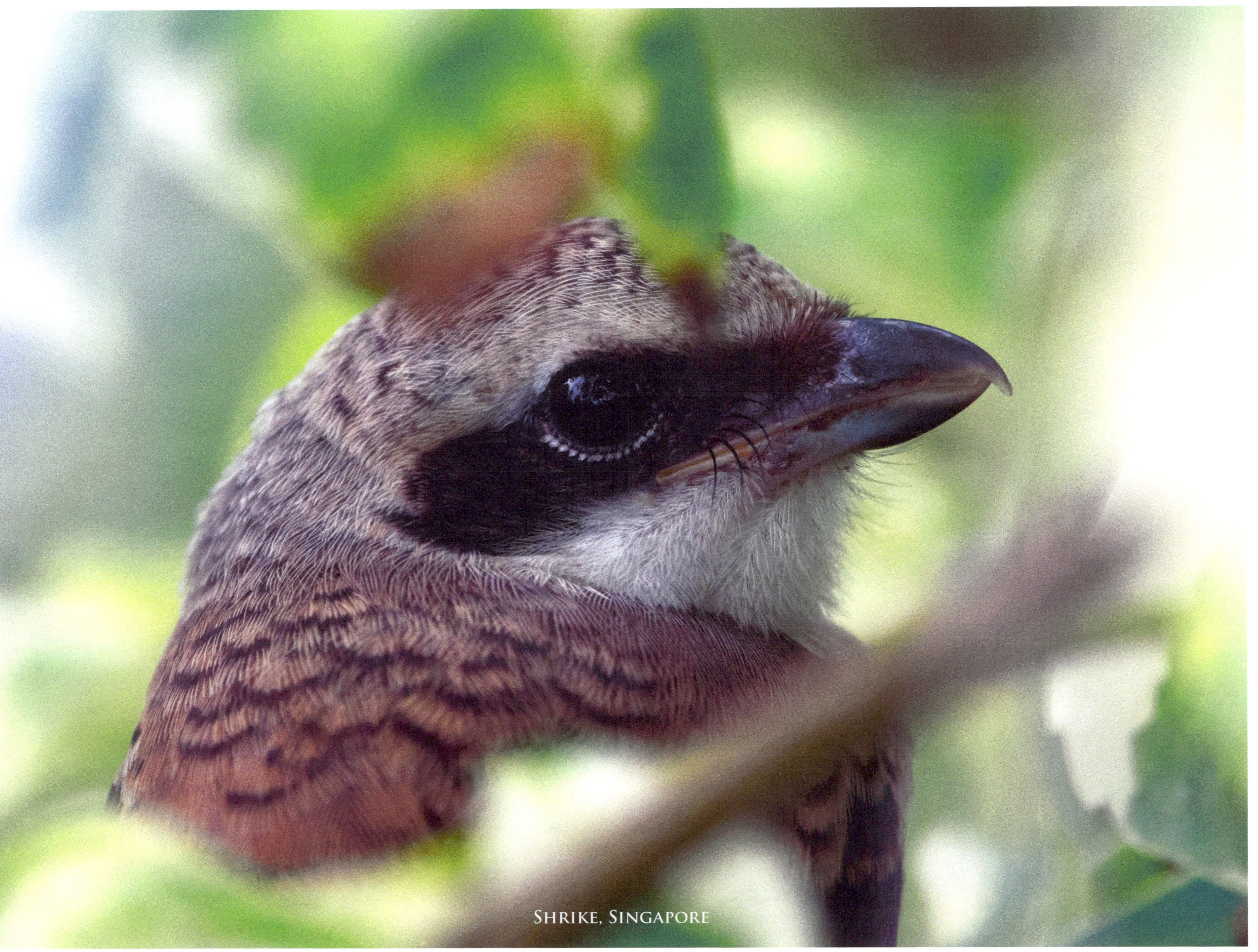

Shrike, Singapore

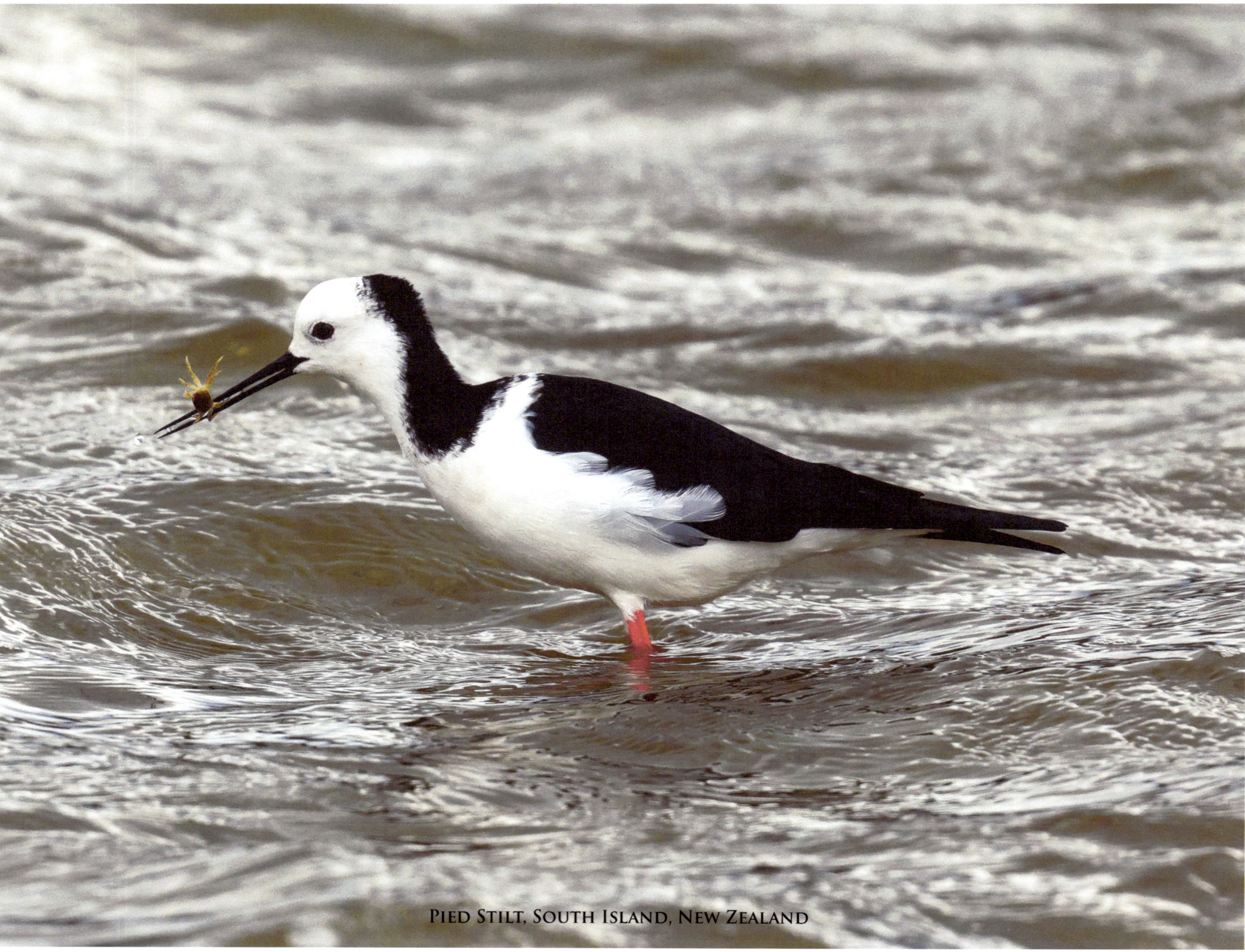

Pied Stilt, South Island, New Zealand

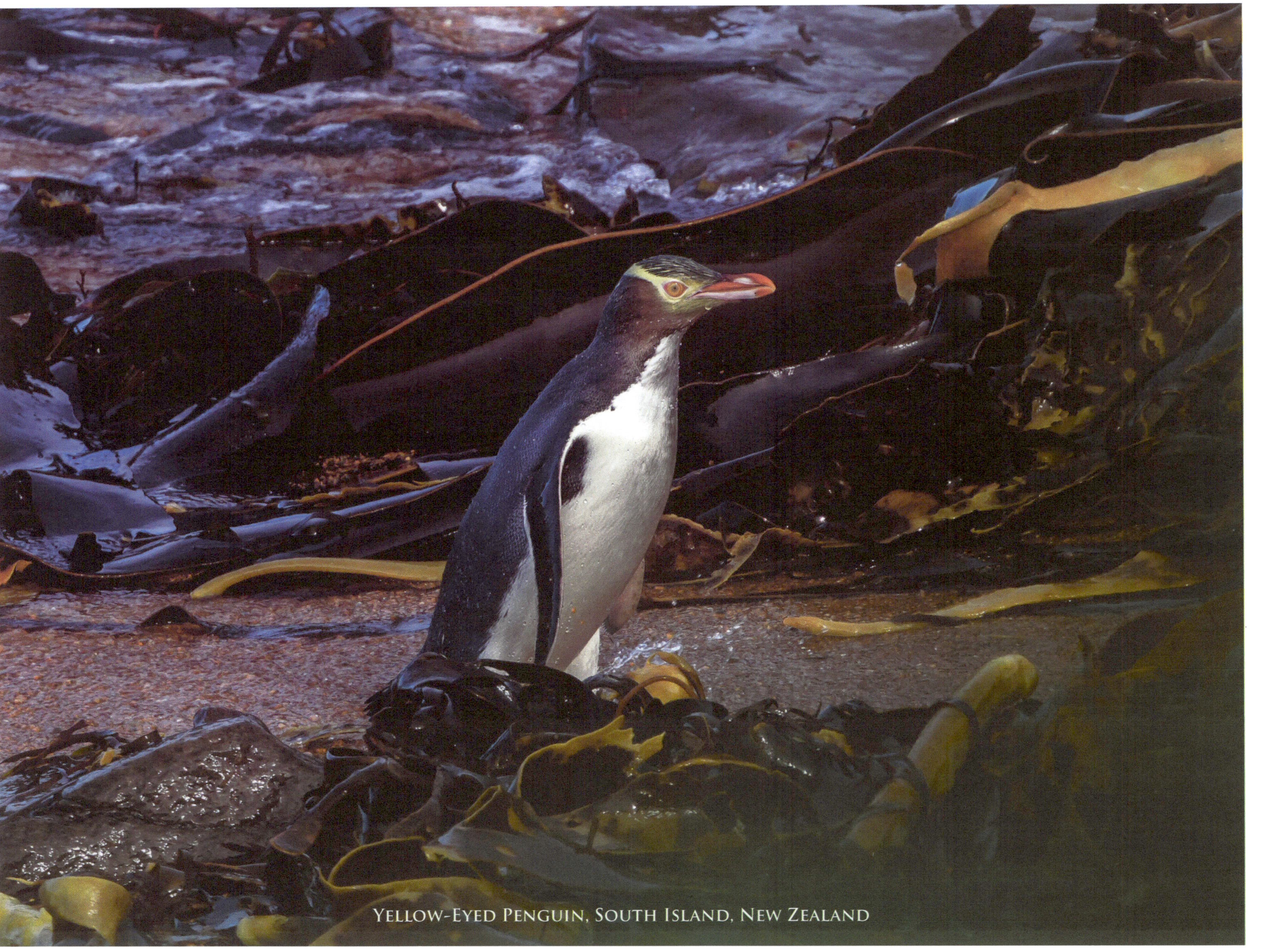

Yellow-Eyed Penguin, South Island, New Zealand

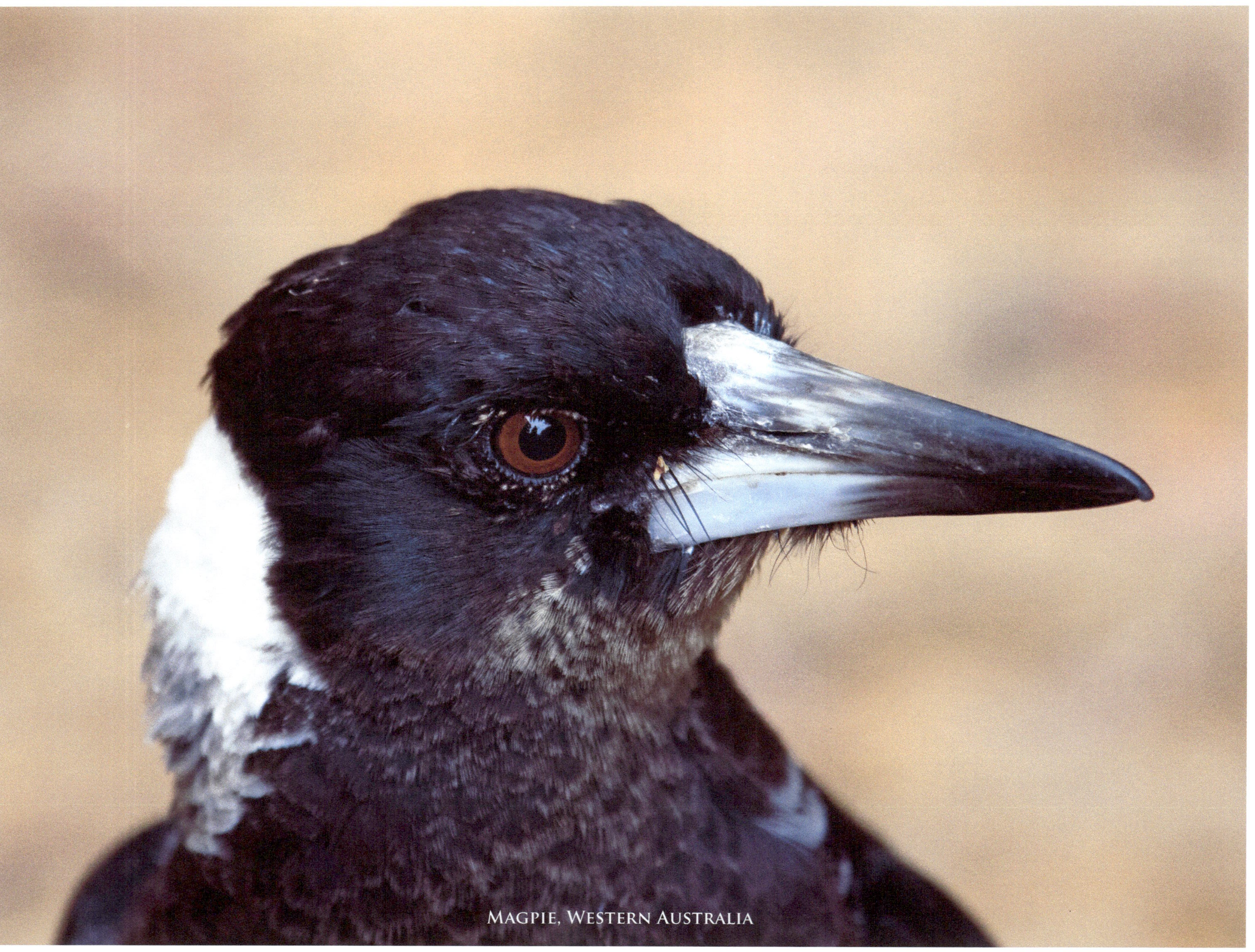

Magpie, Western Australia

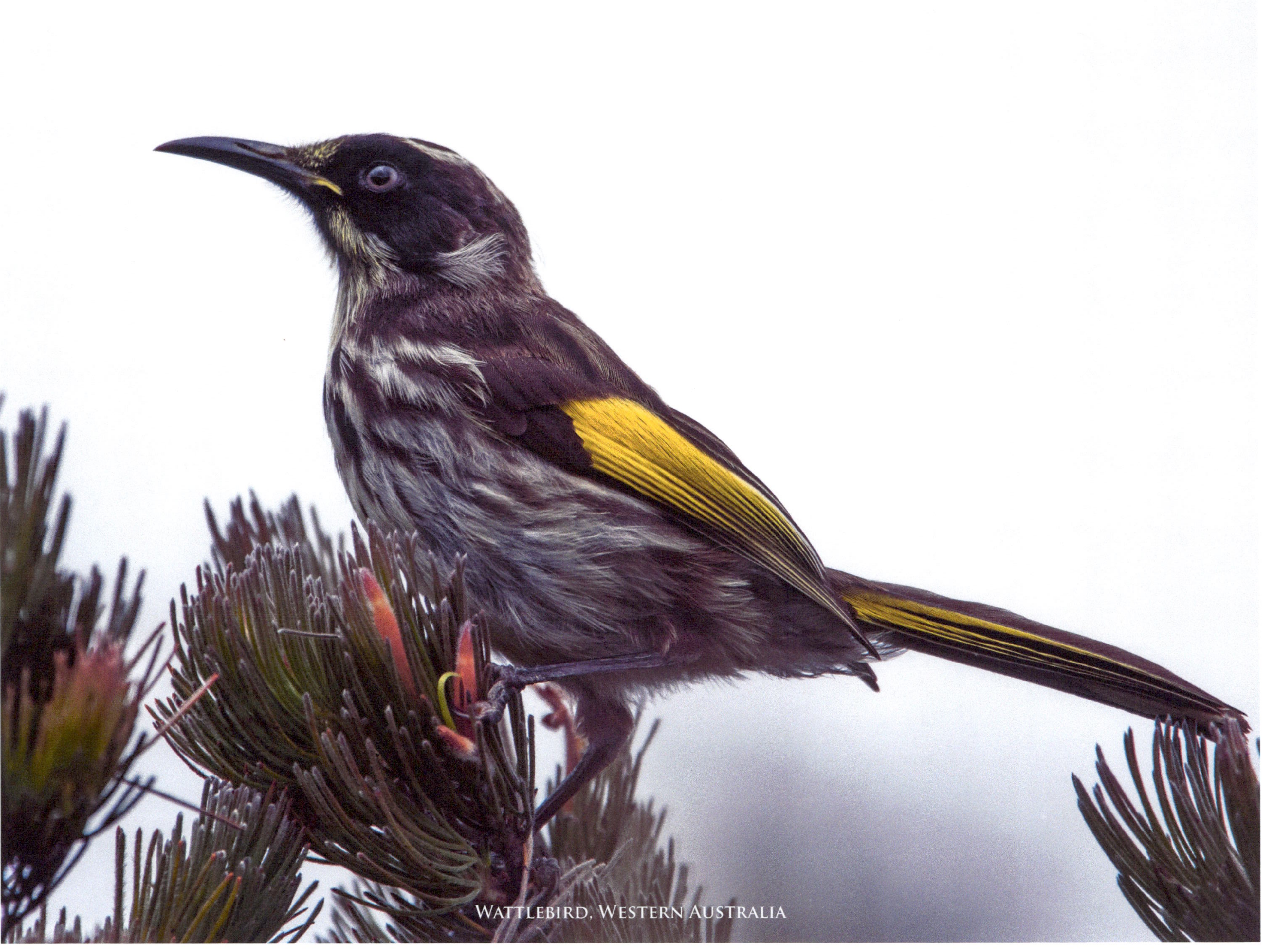

WATTLEBIRD, WESTERN AUSTRALIA

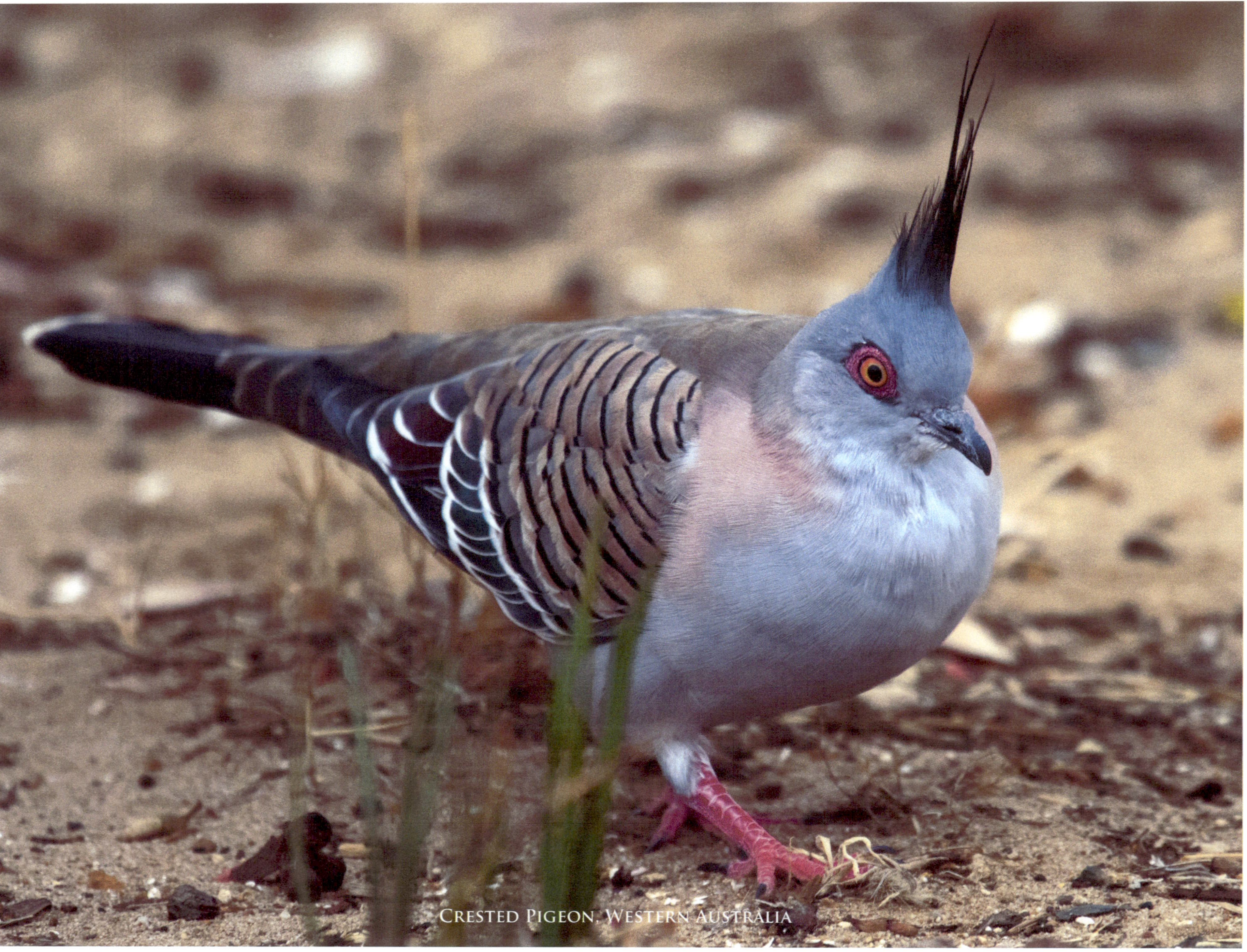

Crested Pigeon, Western Australia

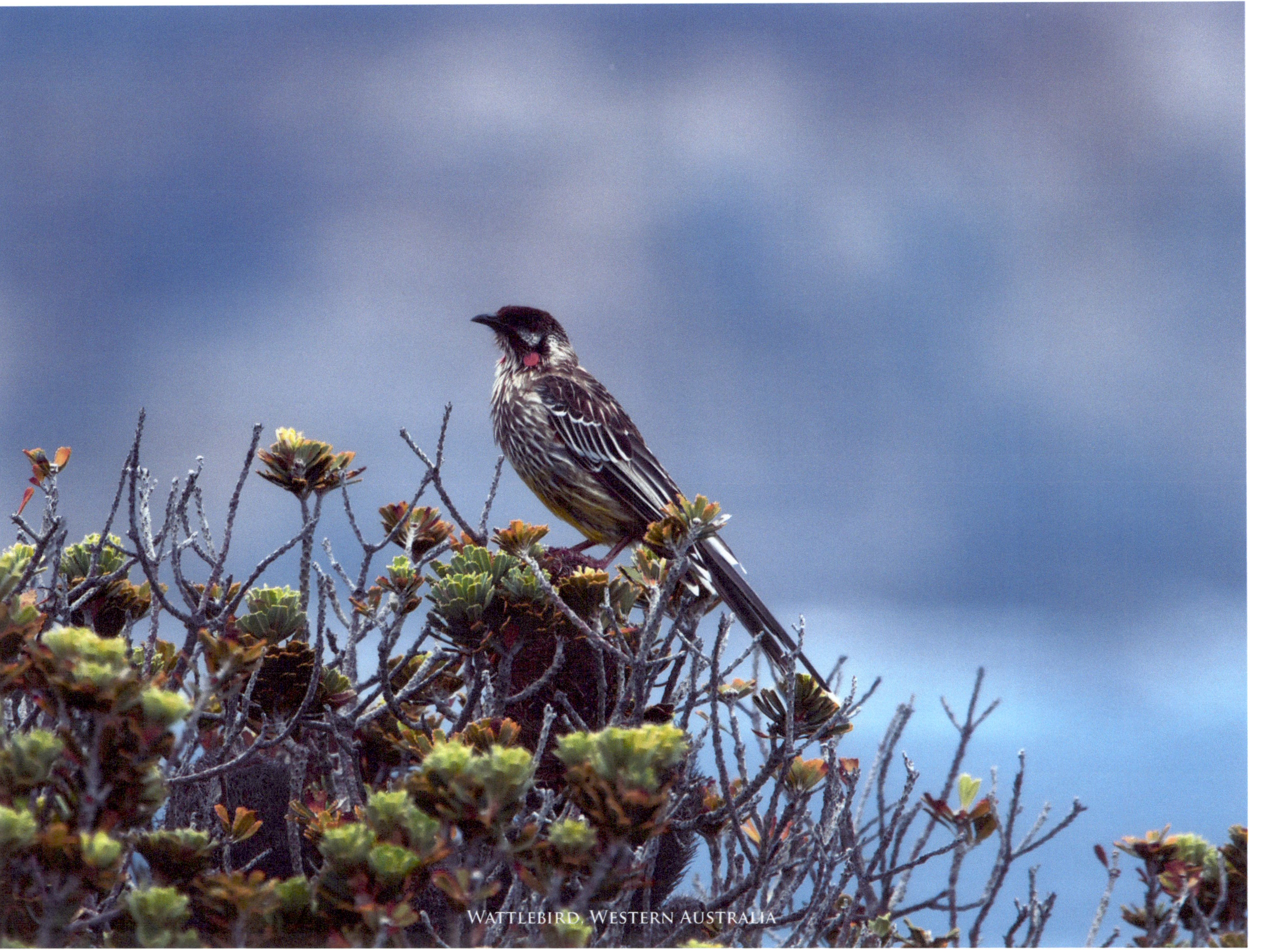

WATTLEBIRD, WESTERN AUSTRALIA

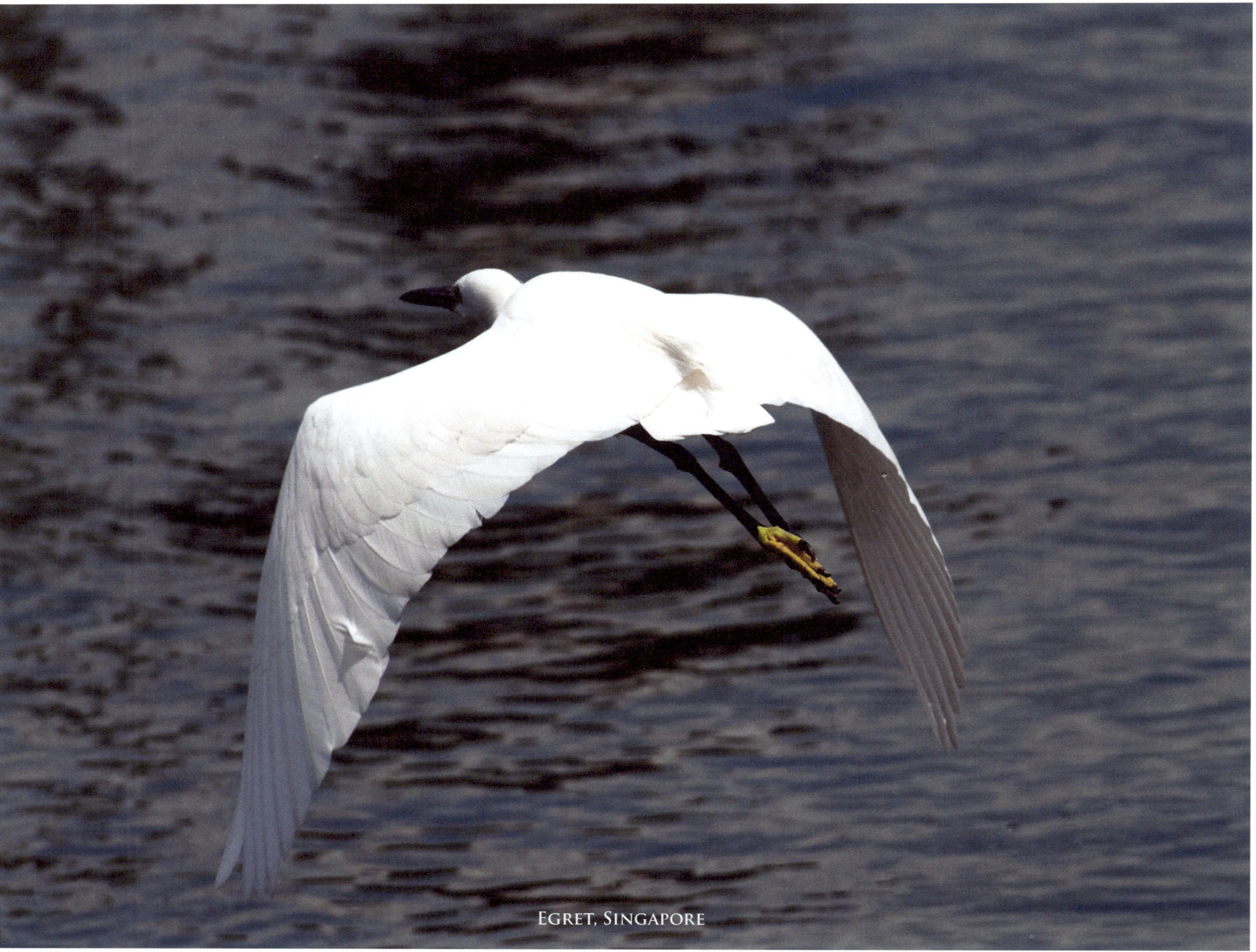

Egret, Singapore

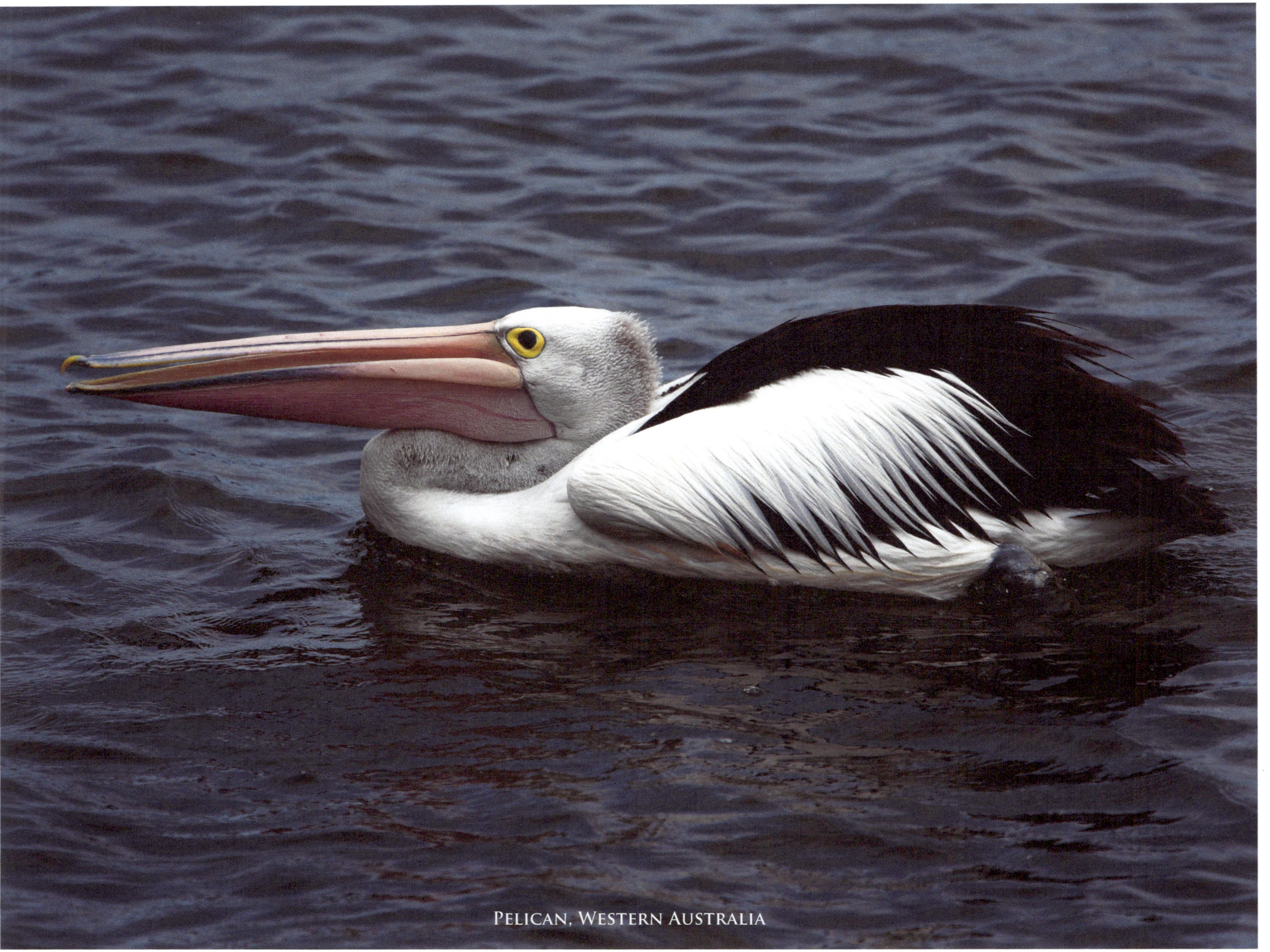

Pelican, Western Australia

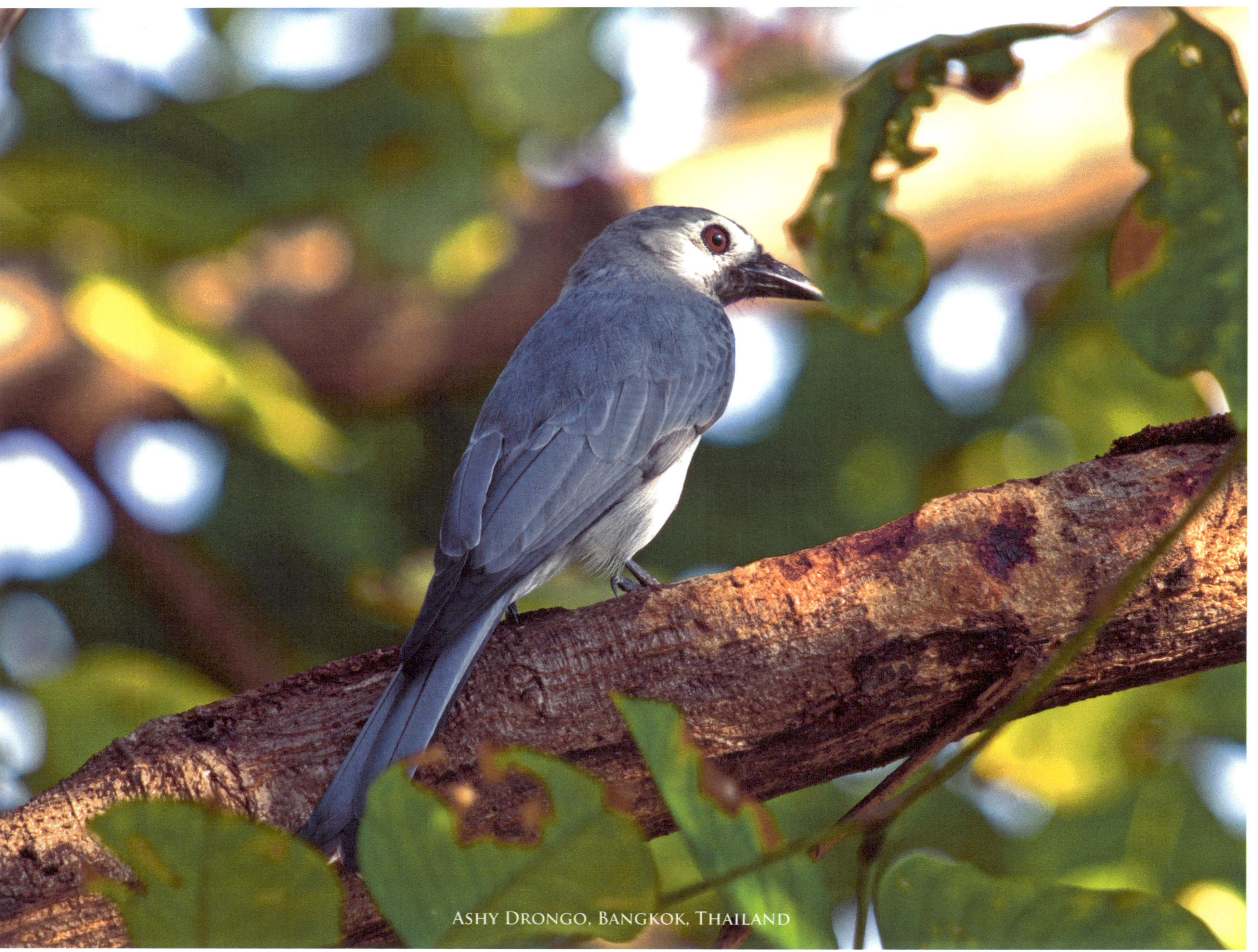

Ashy Drongo, Bangkok, Thailand

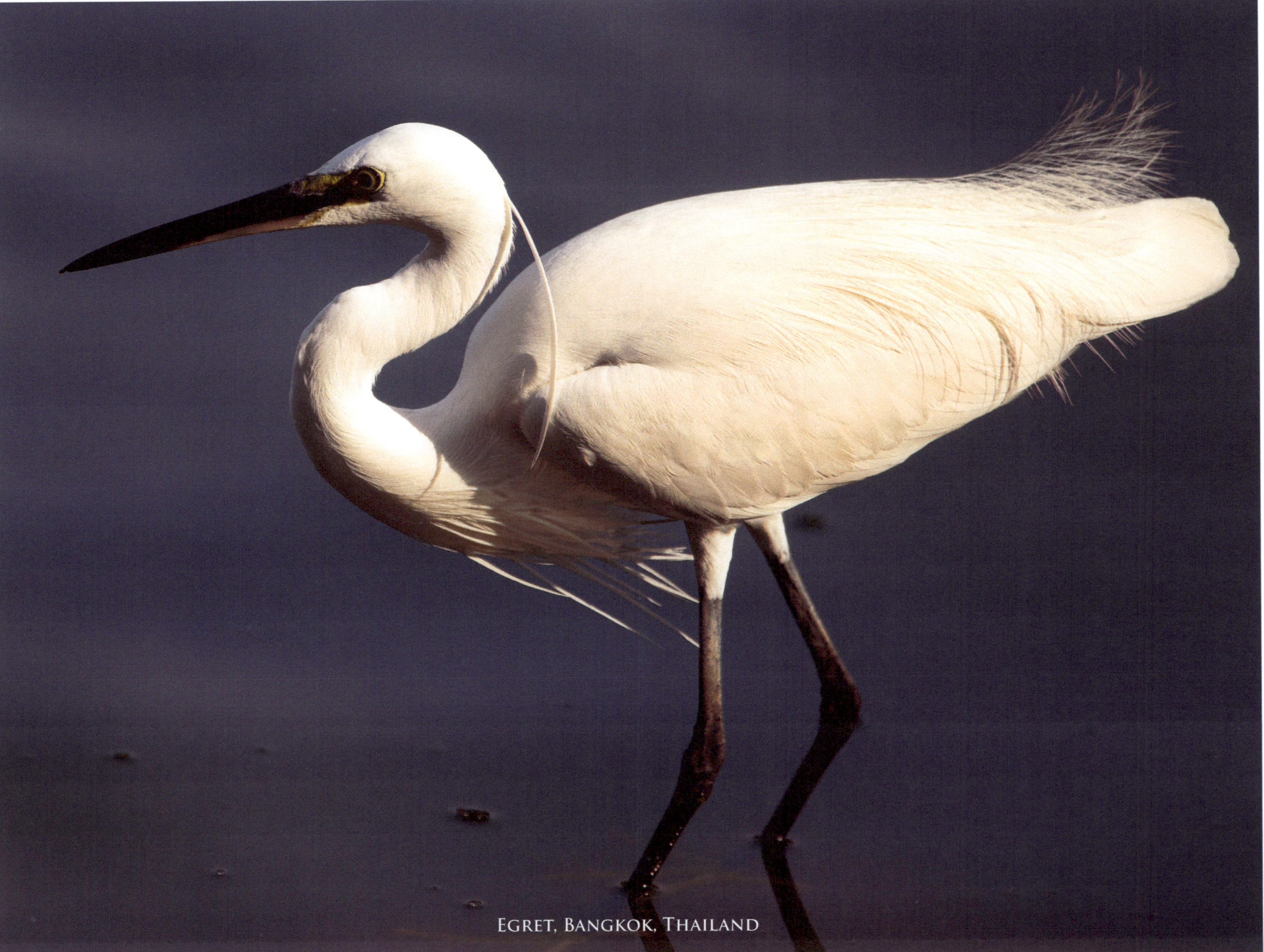

Egret, Bangkok, Thailand

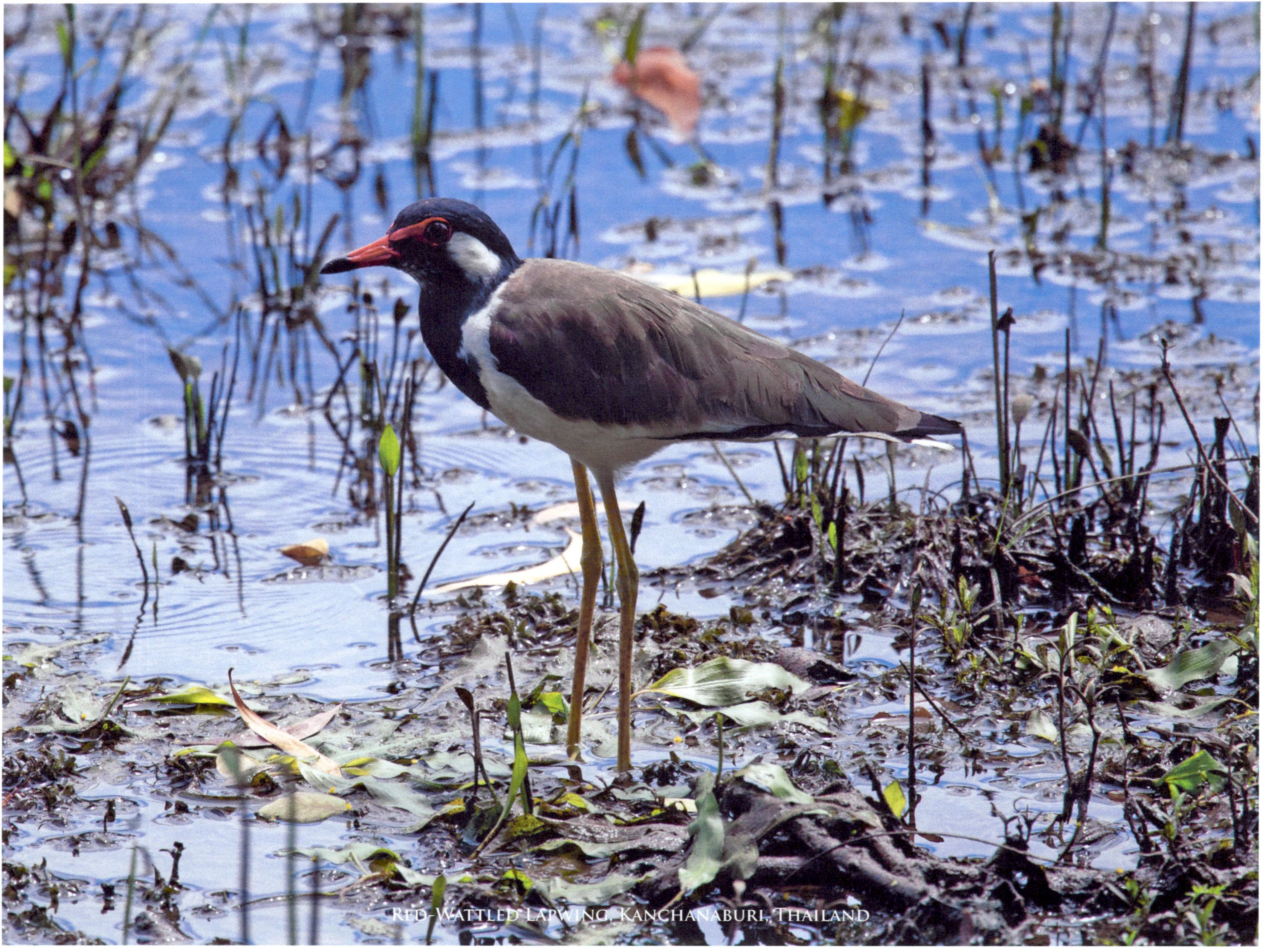

Red-Wattled Lapwing, Kanchanaburi, Thailand

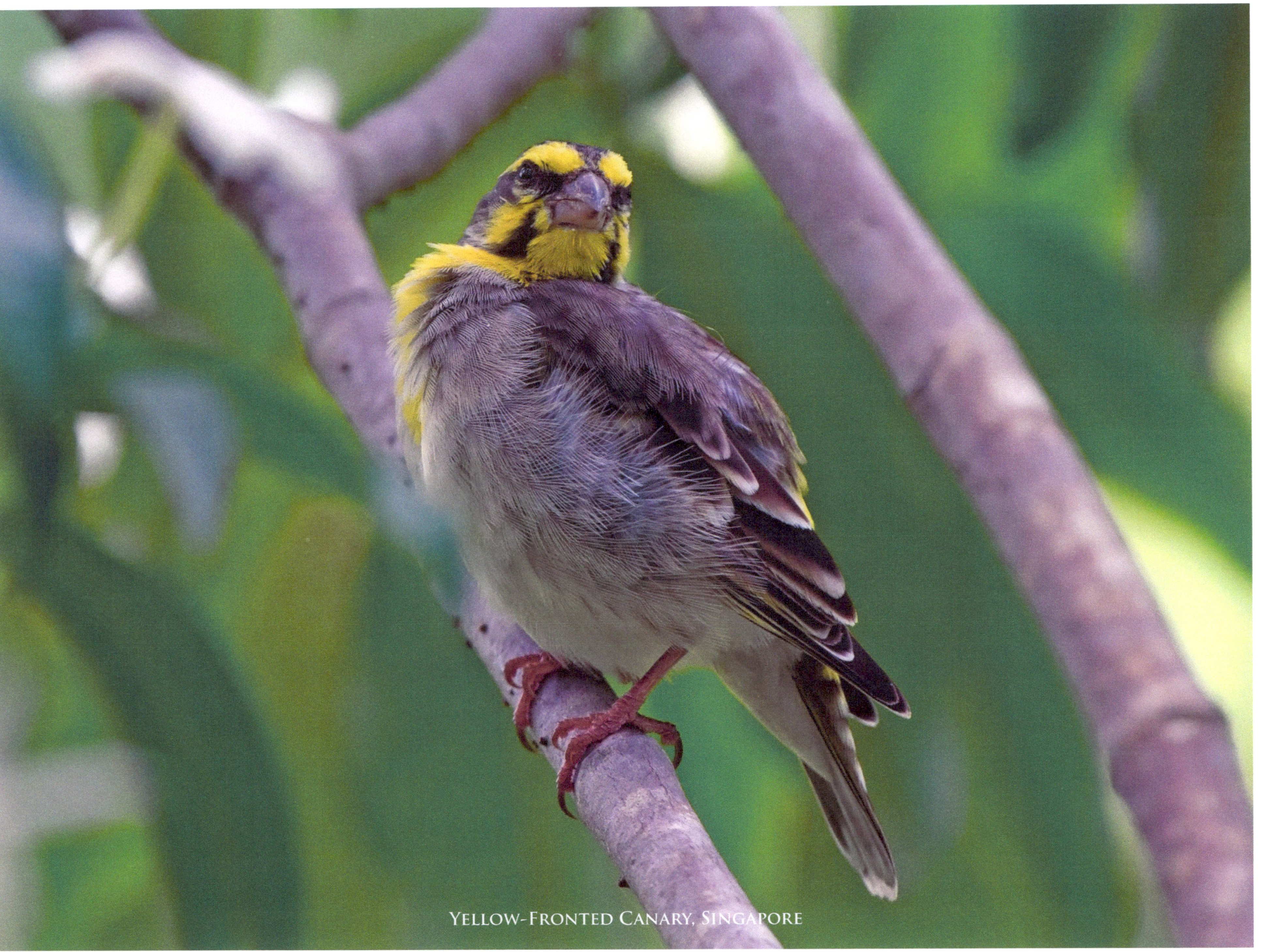

Yellow-Fronted Canary, Singapore

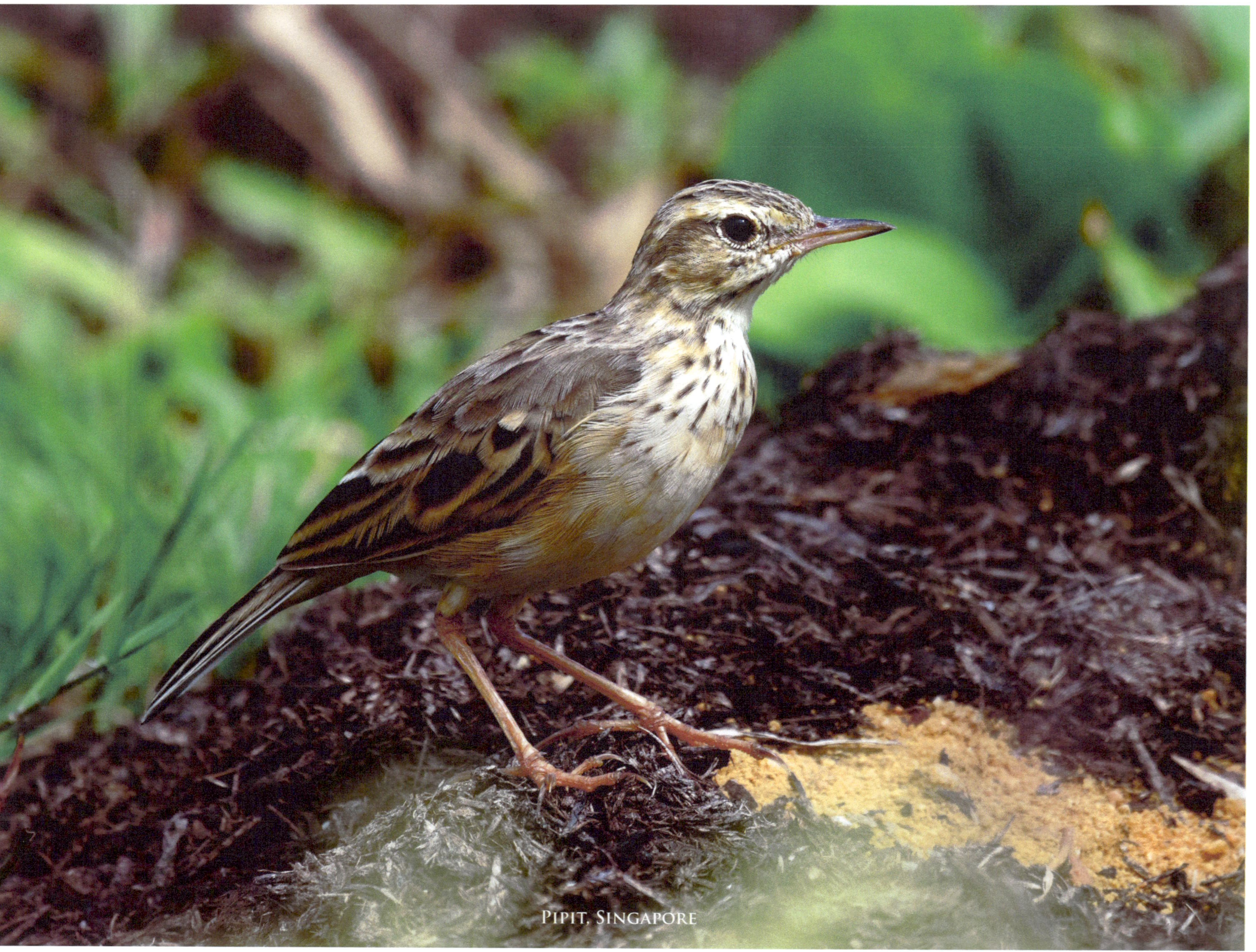

Pipit, Singapore

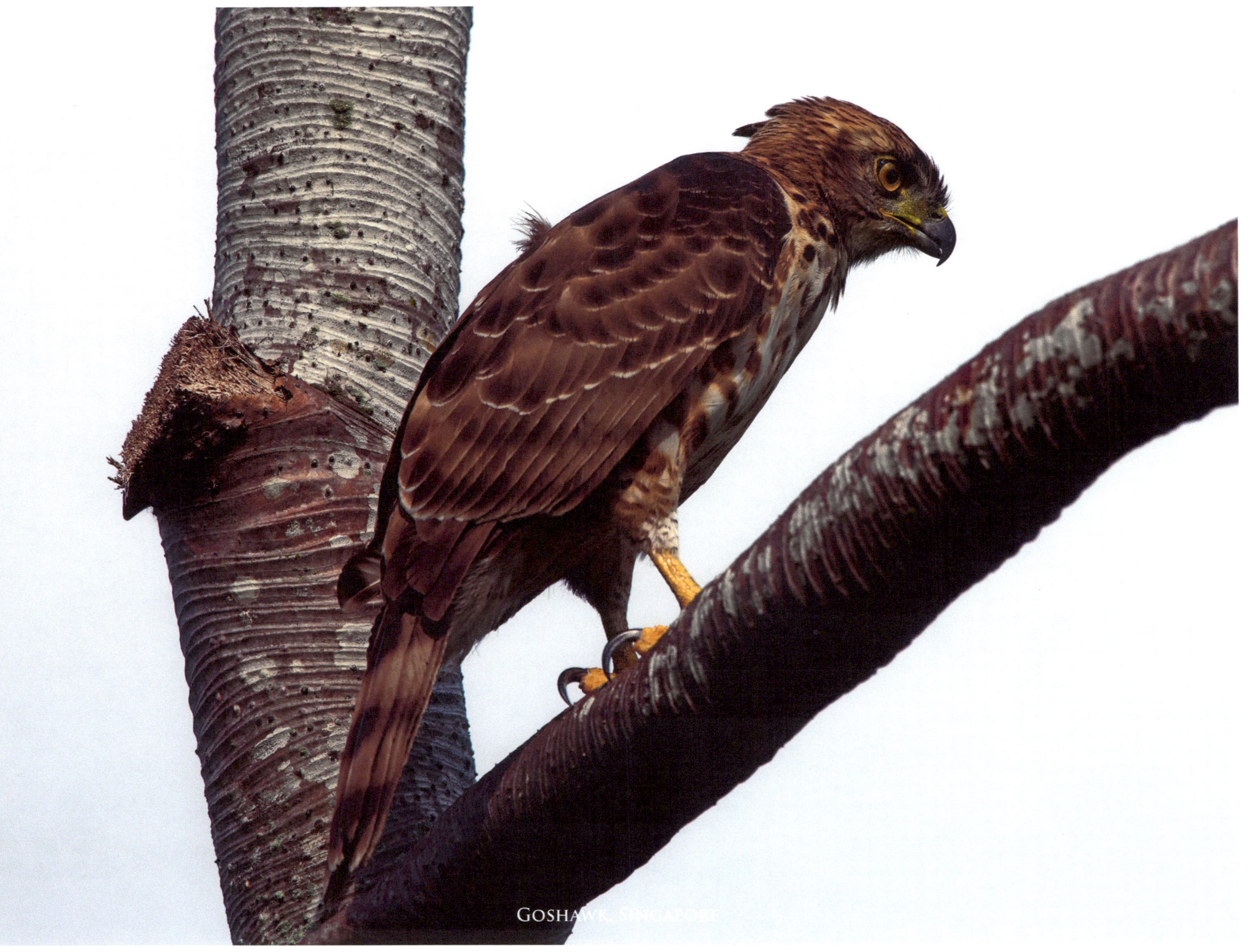

Goshawk, Singapore

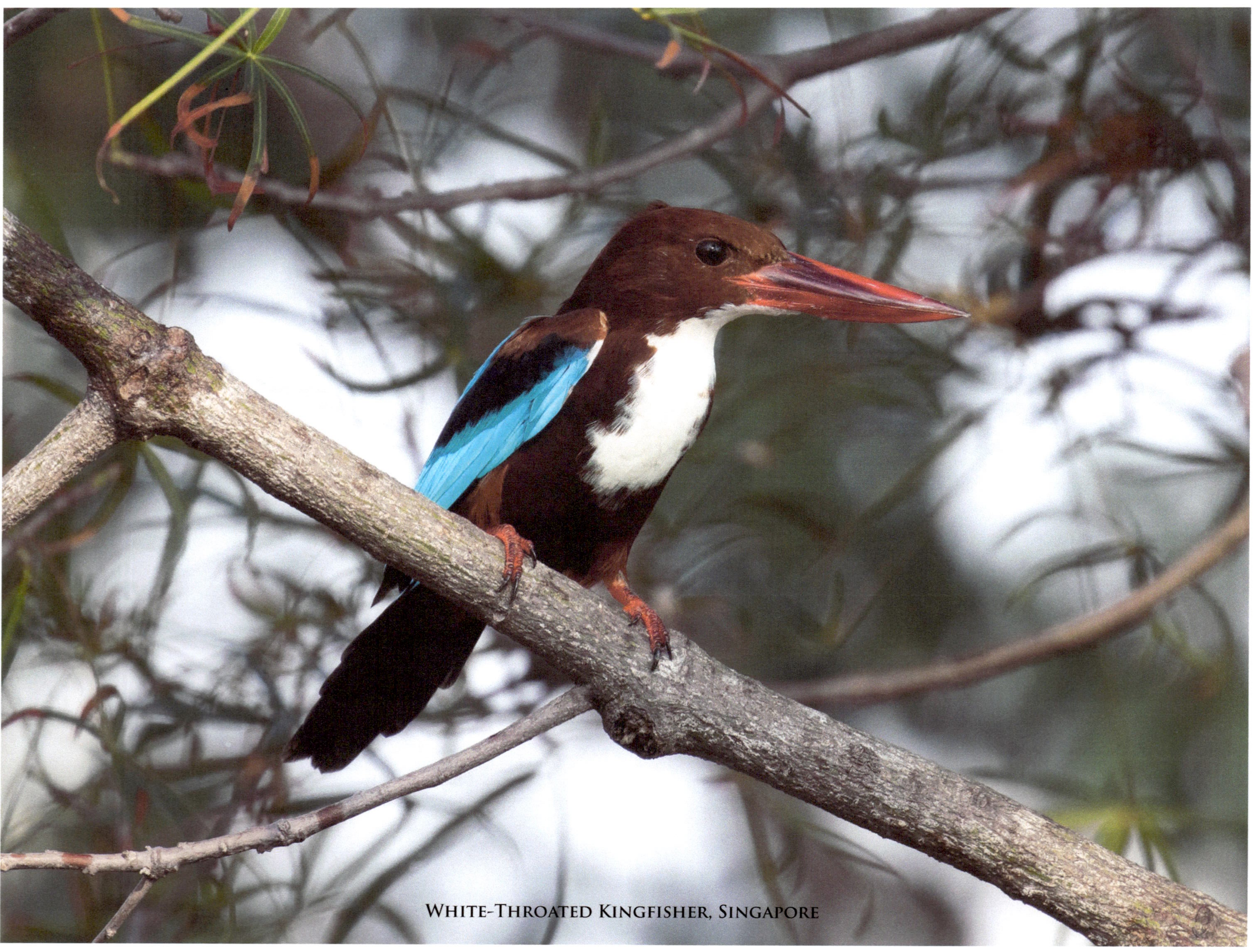

White-Throated Kingfisher, Singapore

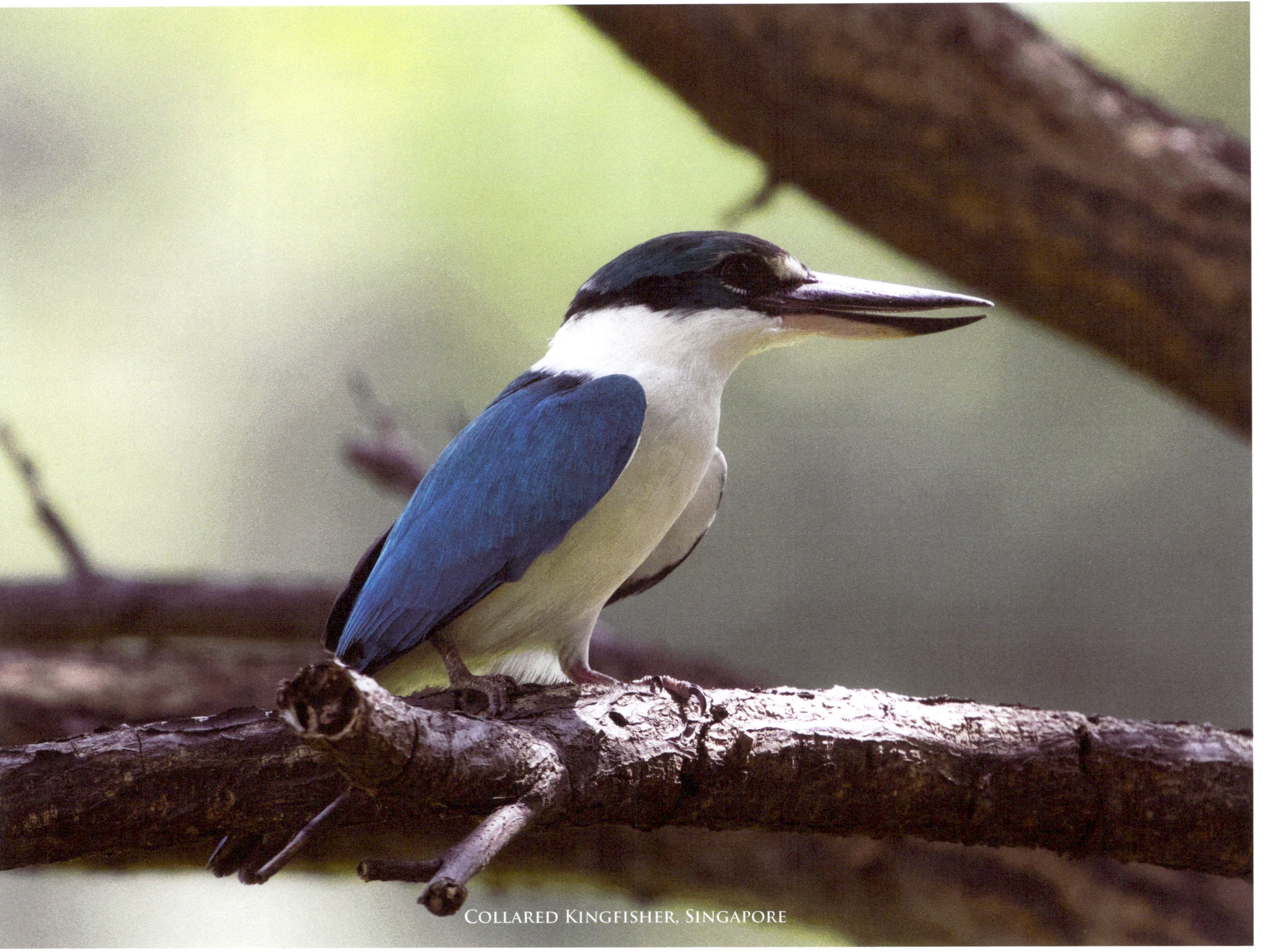

Collared Kingfisher, Singapore

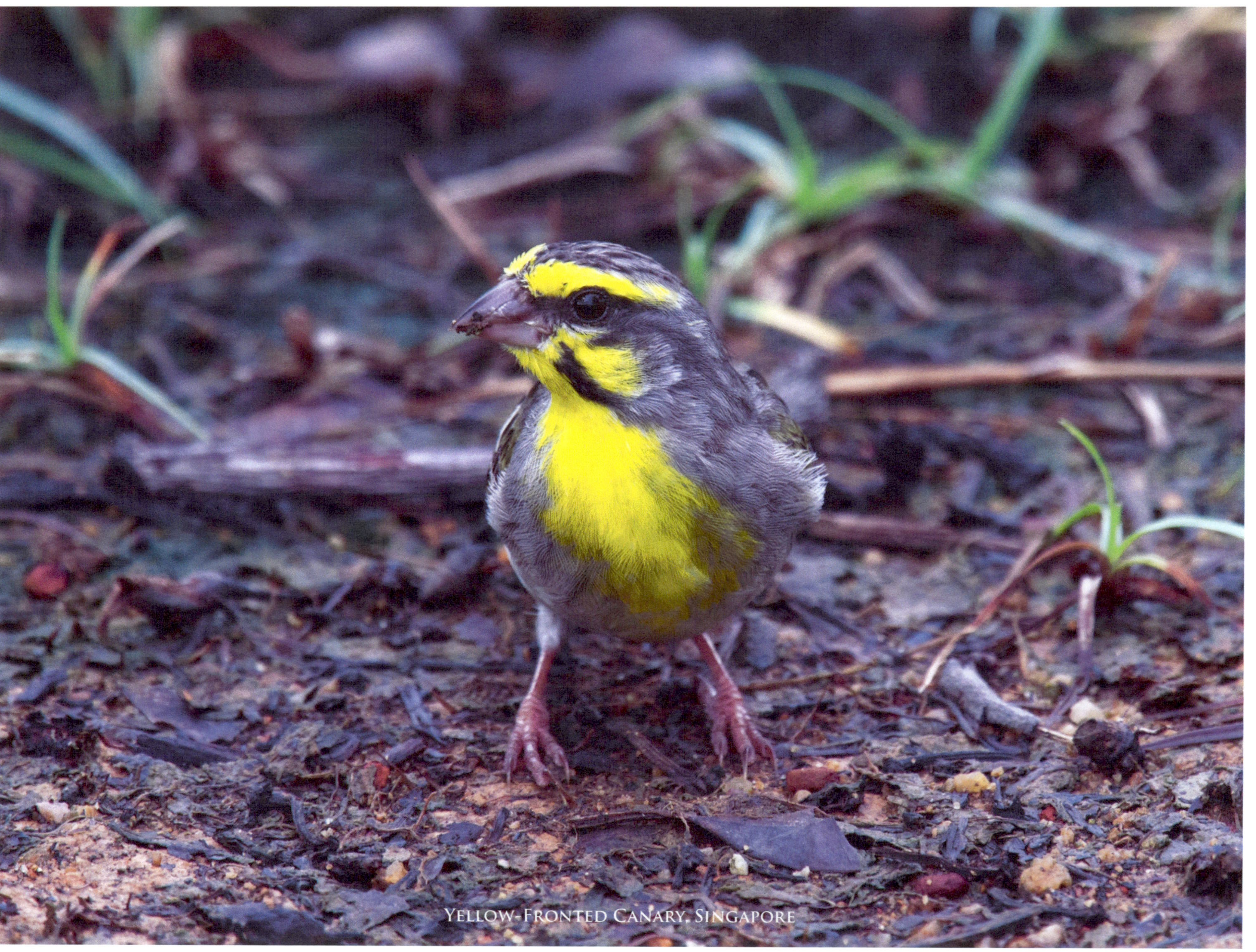

Yellow-Fronted Canary, Singapore

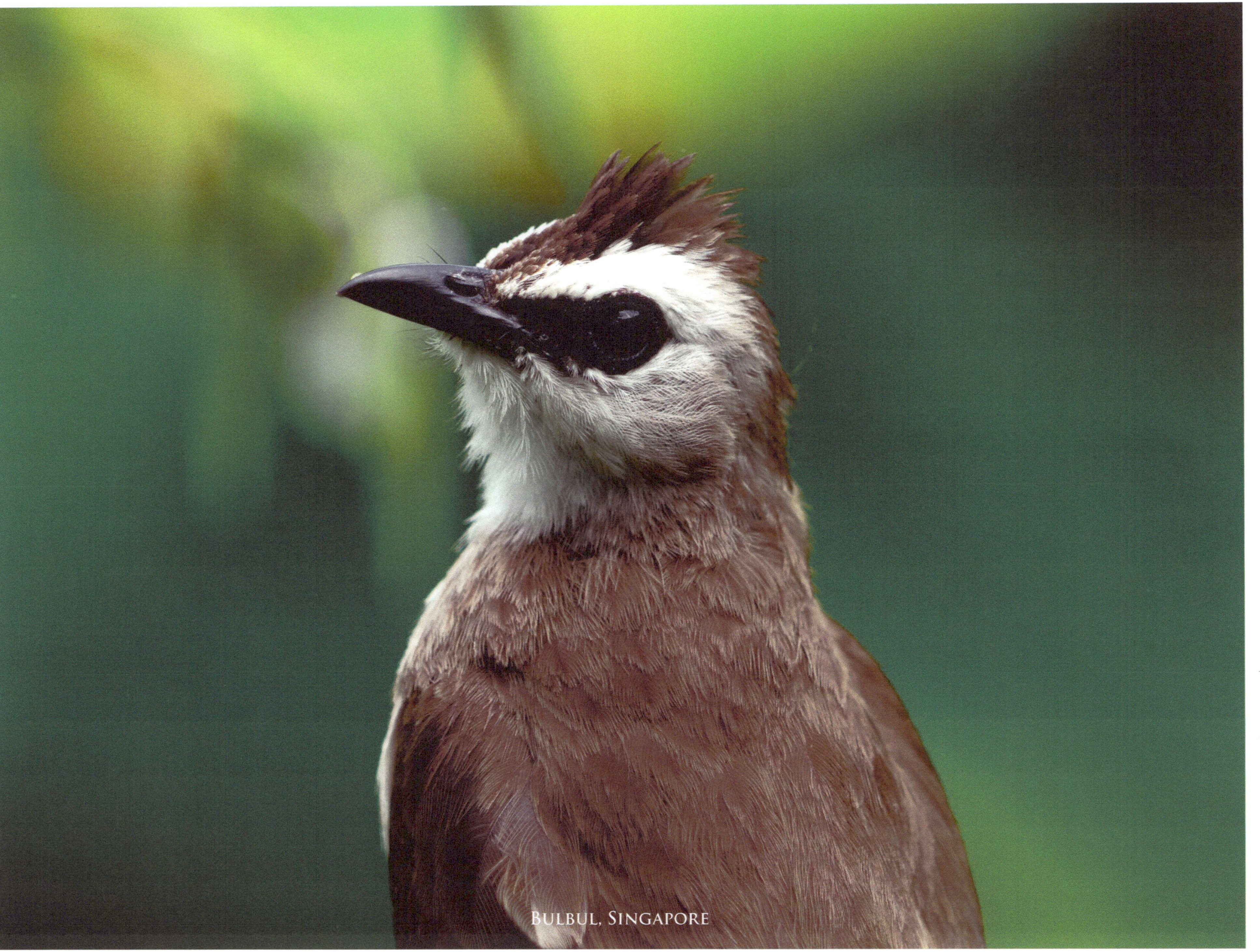

BULBUL, SINGAPORE

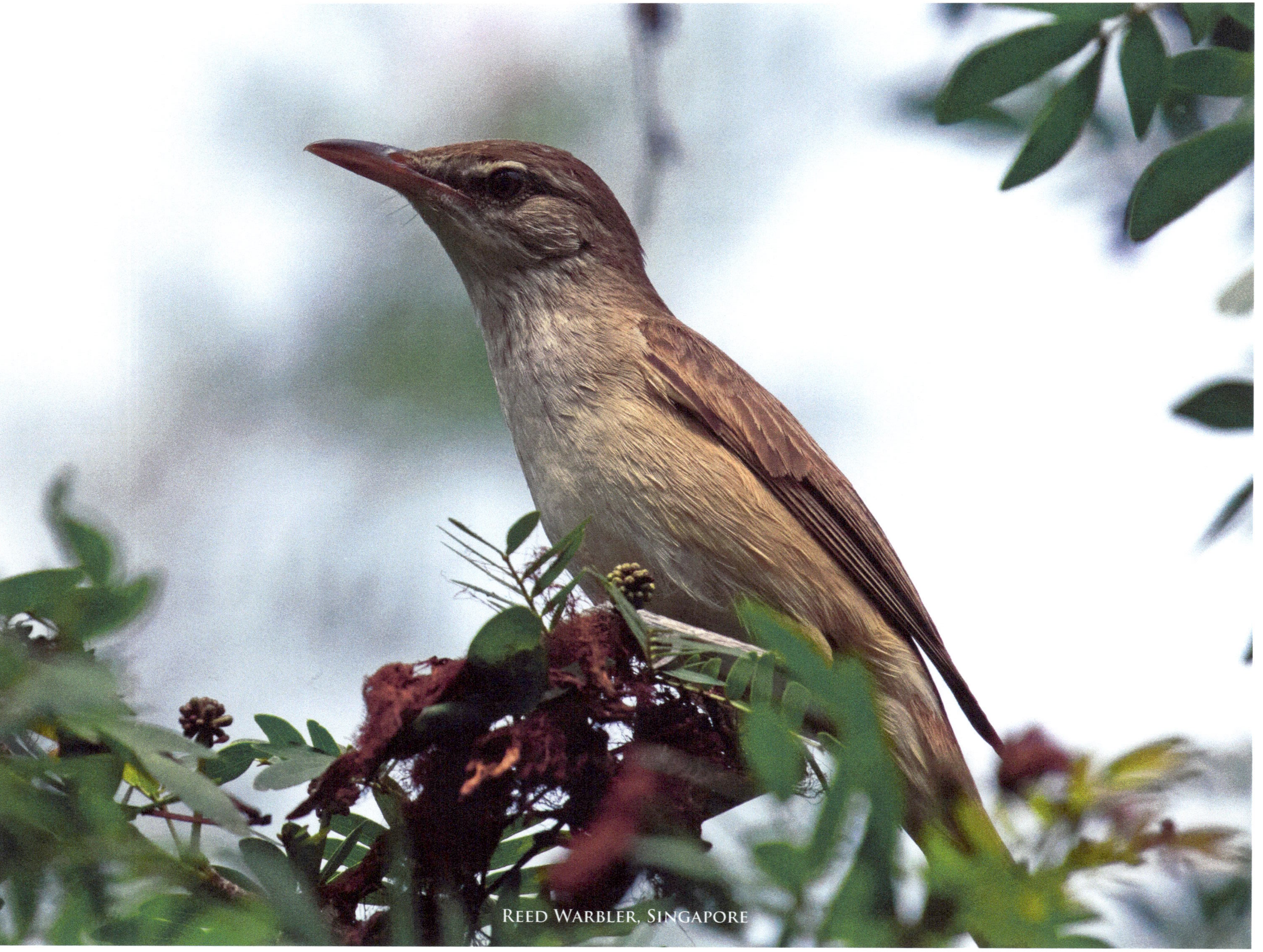

Reed Warbler, Singapore

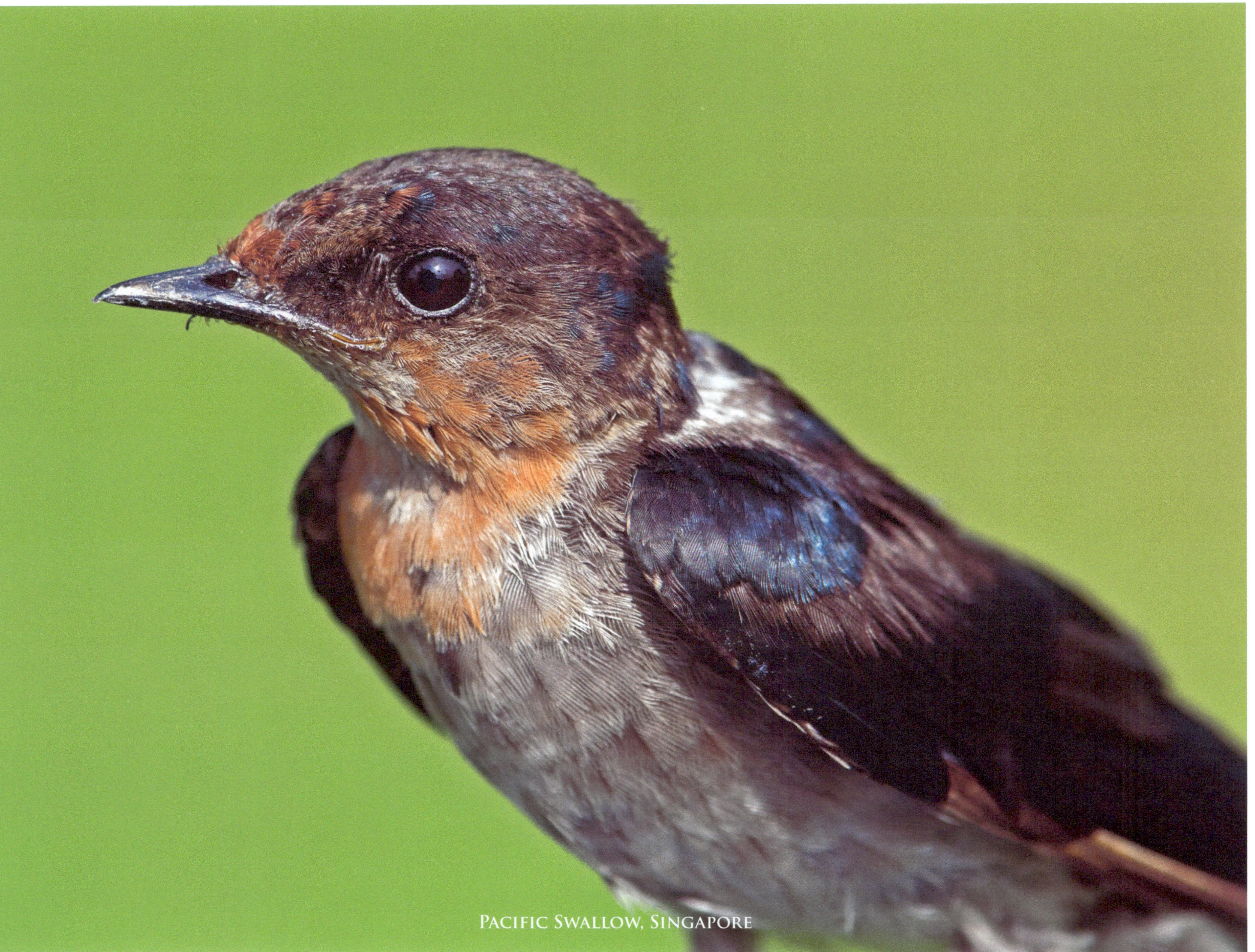

Pacific Swallow, Singapore

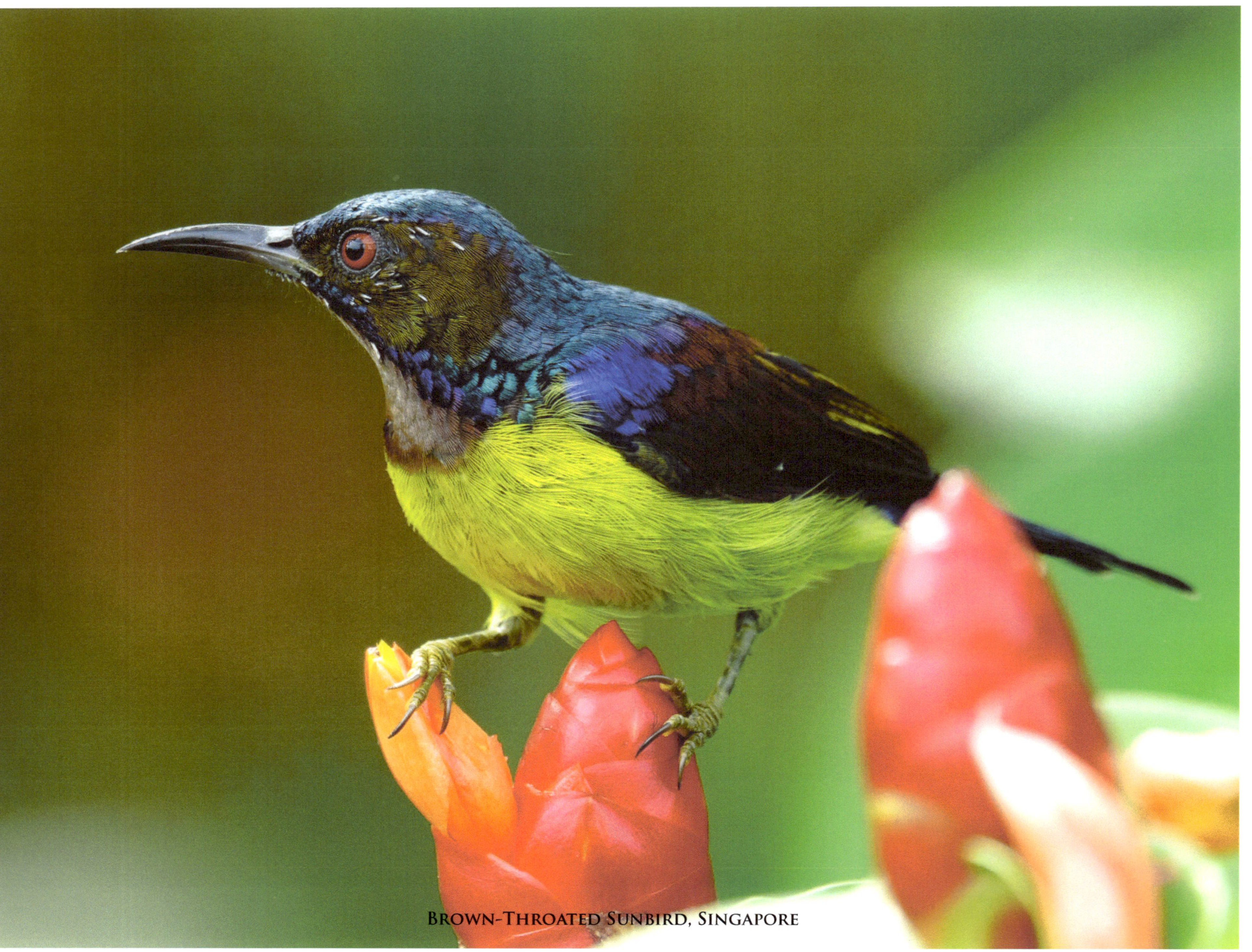

Brown-Throated Sunbird, Singapore

www.ingramcontent.com/pod-product-compliance
Lightning Source LLC
LaVergne TN
LVHW071631100826
845154LV00007BA/131

9780971070271